Contents

Contents

CONTRACT ADMINISTRATION

Gideon Scott Holland

and

Calum Lamont

RICS BOOKS

Acknowledgements

Crown copyright material is reproduced with the permission of the Controller of HMSO and the Queen's Printer for Scotland.

The authors wish to thank Matthew Holt for his help writing this book.

Please note: References to the masculine include, where appropriate, the feminine.

Published by the Royal Institution of Chartered Surveyors (RICS) under the RICS Books imprint
Surveyor Court
Westwood Business Park
Coventry CV4 8JE
UK
www.ricsbooks.com
No responsibility for loss or damage caused to any person acting or refraining from action as a result of the material included in this publication can be accepted by the author or RICS.

ISBN 978 1 84219 317 4

Typeset in Great Britain by Columns Design Ltd, Reading, Berks

Printed in Great Britain by Cromwell Press

Contents

Preface

While chartered surveyors may not need the *breadth* of understanding of the law of their opposite numbers in the legal profession, in a number of key areas of application to construction and property they need a similar *depth* of knowledge. Exactly what the key areas may be depends to some extent on the nature of the surveyor's practice. There are plenty of building surveyors, for example, who know more about the law relating to Party Walls and plenty of quantity surveyors, for example, who know more about construction adjudications, than the average lawyer in general practice.

So surveyors need law and, for a variety of reasons, need to maintain and develop their understanding of it. Changing trends or individual variations in clients' requirements mean that from time to time even the best practitioners (perhaps especially the best practitioners) will feel the need to expand their legal knowledge. The knowledge acquired at college, or in studying for the RICS Assessment of Professional Competence ('APC'), has a limited shelf-life and needs to be constantly updated to maintain its currency. Even specialists working in their areas of expertise need a source of reference as an aide-mémoire or as a first port of call in more detailed research.

The Case in Point Series
RICS Books is committed to meeting the needs of surveying (and other) professionals and the Case in Point series typifies that commitment. It is aimed at those who need to upgrade or update their legal knowledge or who need to have access to a good first reference at the outset of an inquiry. A particular difficulty is the burgeoning of reported decisions of the courts. The sheer scale of the law reports, both general and specialist, makes it very hard even to be aware of recent trends, let alone identify the significance of a particular decision. Thus it was decided to focus on developments in case law.

In any given matter, the practitioner will want to be directed efficiently and painlessly to the decision that bears upon the matter he or she is dealing with; in other words to 'the case in point'. The books in the Case in Point series offer a wealth of legal information which is essential in its practical application to the work of the surveyor or other construction professional. The authors have the high level of expertise required to be selective and succinct, thus achieving a high degree of relevance without sacrificing accessibility. The series has developed incrementally and now forms a collection of specialist handbooks which can deliver what practitioners need – the law on the matter they are handling, when they want it.

Contract Administration by Gideon Scott Holland and Calum Lamont
The original rationale for the existence of a contract administrator was simple. A person was needed to undertake routine procedures called for either expressly or impliedly by the contract, such as ordering variations to the design or giving other instructions as they became necessary. The client needed to know that the decisions were made properly, particularly when in accepting or approving completed work or admitting a claim for loss and expense, they led directly to a payment by the client to the contractor. Decision-making, particularly in relation to disputes and potential disputes, has always been at the heart of the role. Chapter 13 of the book contains cases detailing the modern position in this respect.

In former times, candidates for the role would have been few. Until well after World War II, most contractors largely lacked the capacity for management, especially of a legally defined process and even today their immediate financial interest would, in the mind of the owner, disqualify them from any involvement in contract administration.

But clients too lacked the sophistication and the inclination to run a project; often they still do.

Frequently, the only serious candidate a hundred years ago, or even fifty, was the designer of the works, the architect or engineer. No one would know the project better and no one else would combine the necessary literacy and numeracy which came with a professional education and experience of the processes of design and construction.

This practical choice became enshrined in the Standard Form of Contracts, in the RIBA Forms (latterly JCT) the architect became the Architect and in the ICE forms, the engineer became the Engineer.

These terms are not exhaustive; other contracts referred to the Quantity Surveyor or the Superintending Officer (SO) and, as different procurement models, contract administration might be in the hands of the Construction Manager, or, notably under the New Engineering Contract (NEC) forms, the Project Manager.

The extent of the role and the scope of its attendant powers and duties are thus partly defined by the contract itself, even though the contract administrator is not a party to it. They will also be defined by the conditions of engagement between architect/engineer and client and their express and implied contents.

Given this contractual basis, to which must be added the possibility of duties of care in tort, it is not surprising that contract administration has generated a large and important body of case law. It is extremely important that this should be understood by contractors who have to deal with them, by clients who depend upon them and above all by the contract administrators themselves.

The chapters in this book on instructions, information, variations and waivers (chapter 4), extensions of time – liquidated damages and loss and expense (chapter 5) and valuation certification and termination (chapter 6) emphasise the significance of correct procedure. That significance can hardly be overstated. To take one example of a dozen available, incorrect application of the extension of time machinery of the contract would be likely to bring into play the *Peak v McKinney* prevention principle, by which the client would lose the right to claim liquidated damages for late delivery.

What is at stake in contract administration has led, inevitably, to a further body of case law on the liability of the professionals themselves to their clients and even to third parties, chapters 2 and 3 on project management and supervision respectively deal amongst other things with the new cases on liability of project managers such as *Pride Valley Foods v Hall & Partners* and the *Royal Brompton* case, and the 'supervision versus inspection liability' issue in *Alexander Corfield v Grant* and *Consarc Design v Hutch*. Chapters 9, 10 and 11 are on contractual and tortious duties, duty of care and limitation. Conversely, the duties owed *to* the contract administrators, including rights to payment, are in chapter 12.

To marshall and analyse the large body of case law on contract administration, including a few key overseas decisions which have influenced the development of English law, has required a high degree of expertise, as well as industry. Both authors are barristers from specialist construction set Keating Chambers, recently named Construction Set of the Year 2006 at the Chambers & Partners Bar Awards.

Gideon Scott Holland was called to the Bar in 1999 and has established himself as a successful practitioner in construction, following several Technology and Construction Court cases with a recent appearance in the Court of Appeal in *Yorkshire Water Services v Taylor Woodrow Construction*. He has contributed to a number of publications in the field, principally on building contracts.

Calum Lamont was called to the Bar in 2004 after a Double First at Cambridge. He has advised in a number of significant construction disputes and recently appeared in the Technology and Construction Court in *All-in-One Building v Makers UK Ltd*. He is co-author of the Building Defects title in the RICS Case in Point Series.

Together, they have made an important addition to the published material available to surveying and construction professionals concerned with the administration of contracts.

Anthony Lavers, 2006.
Visiting Professor of Law, Oxford Brookes University.
Consultant Editor, Case in Point Series.

List of Acts and Statutory Instruments

The following Acts and Statutory Instruments are referenced in this publication.

Arbitration Act 1979
Civil Liability (Contribution) Act 1978
Compensation Act 2006
Contracts (Rights of Third Parties) Act 1999
Defective Premises Act 1972
Housing Grants, Construction and Regeneration Act 1996
Latent Damage Act 1986
Law Reform (Contributory Negligence) Act 1945
Limitation Act 1980
London Building Act 1894
Unfair Terms in Consumer Contract Regulations 1999

The text of this publication is divided into commentary and case summaries. The commentary is enclosed between grey highlighted lines for ease of reference.

Table of cases

PART 1:
Introduction

1
Contracts and their administrators

1.1 INTRODUCTION

Contract administrators, regardless of their professional background, will invariably find themselves in a unique position in relation to the construction project in question, irrespective of the form of contract they administer. Even though they are engaged by the employer to carry out a variety of tasks (whether prior to, during, or after the completion of works), they must nevertheless act fairly and exercise independent judgment when it comes to addressing their decision-making functions under a building contract.

Events will occur which trigger the operation of certain contractual provisions in respect of which the employer and contractor will often have interests or expectations which are diametrically opposed. For example, if a project falls into delay, the contractor will naturally seek an extension of time in order to protect himself from liquidated damages; the employer, on the other hand, will be desirous of achieving completion and possession as soon as possible and is unlikely to be willing to sanction further payments to a dilatory contractor. The impartiality of the contract administrator's judgment becomes especially critical when the form of contract in question provides that his decision will be final and conclusive.

As a result, a contract administrator can perhaps be forgiven for approaching his role on any particular project somewhat cautiously. However, the central point to remember is that the duties of a contract administrator will depend in all cases on the particular facts and the terms of his retainer. Nevertheless, it is possible to give a general list of the sort of duties that might be expected. Such a list was drawn up by the editor of

3

Hudson's Building Contracts in 1926 and it is suggested that it is still fairly comprehensive. The list is:

1   to advise and consult with the employer (not as a lawyer) as to any limitation which may exist as to the use of the land to be built on, either (*inter alia*) by restrictive covenants or by the rights of adjoining owners or the public over the land, or by statutes and bye-laws affecting the works to be executed;

2   to examine the site, sub-soil and surroundings;

3   to consult with and advise the employer as to the proposed work;

4   to prepare sketch plans and a specification having regard to all the conditions which exist and to submit them to the employer for approval, with an estimate of the probable cost, if requested;

5   to elaborate and, if necessary, modify or amend the sketch plans as he may be instructed and prepare working drawings and a specification or specifications;

6   to consult with and advise the employer as to obtaining tenders, whether by invitation or by advertisement, and as to the necessity or otherwise of employing a quantity surveyor (engineers do not often employ a quantity surveyor);

7   to supply the builder with copies of the contract drawings and specification, supply such further drawings and give such instructions as may be necessary, supervise the work, and see that the contractor performs the contract, and advise the employer if he commits any serious breach thereof;

8   to perform his duties to his employer as defined by any contract with his employer or by the contract with the builder, and generally to act as the employer's agent in all matters connected with the work and the contract, except where otherwise prescribed by the contract with the builder, as, for instance, in cases where he has under the contract to act as arbitrator or quasi-arbitrator.

1.2   EXAMPLES OF TYPICAL PROVISIONS

The RICS 1988 Guidance Notes for 'Project Management: Construction Monitoring' describe the functions of a project manager in the following terms:

1   identifying the client's requirements;

2   assembling a project team;

3   developing a programme of works from planning to post-construction;

4   establishing a budget;

5   arranging, where agreed, capital and life cycle costs studies;

6   liaison on legal matters;

7   determining and implementing the tender process;

8   preparing cash-flow forecasts and statements and authorising payments;

9   continuously reviewing the programme to correct deviations and apprise the client of their occurrence;

10 establishing a management framework and procedures;

11 co-ordination of construction work in person or through an agent;

12 monitoring performance and progress;

13 quality control by inspection and/or arranging third party insurance for Quality Assurance schemes;

14 reviewing all payments due under contracts and finance agreement;

15 handing over the building after re-testing and full commissioning of services;

16 dealing with defects during defects liability period and providing agreed management of relocation.

The project manager on any given project may be required to carry out any or all of these functions. On larger projects, the project manager's principal functions will be management and liaison related whereas on smaller projects he may supervise the contract works himself. The project manager may be appointed under a standard form or, more typically, a bespoke contract.

ACE Conditions of Engagement 1995 Agreement E

The ACE Conditions of Engagement 1995 Agreement E defines the obligations of the Project Manager in the following terms:

1   The Project Manager performs the Normal Services as follows:

   - Inception
   - Briefing
   - Organisation and Communication
   - Management of Contracts (for both consultants and contractors)
   - Consultation and approvals
   - Programme control
   - Cost management
   - Management of technical coordination
   - Quality management
   - Risk management
   - Health and Safety
   - Commissioning and Occupation

2   The Project Manager performs any of these Additional Services where requested by the client:

   - Preparation of a business case
   - Work following a client's decision to seek parliamentary powers
   - Work linked to any application necessary for the project to proceed
   - Preparation of any information for the client's negotiations
   - Obtaining any necessary information
   - Work linked to feasibility recommendations
   - Risk management plan
   - Agreement of variation valuations
   - Negotiation of contracts/sub-contracts
   - Periodic site visits
   - Issuing of certificates
   - Factoring time into programme for performance testing
   - Work linked to any claim/dispute
   - Examination of any financial claim

– Insurance liaison

The Project Manager is to ensure that legal, professional and financial services are undertaken by others and to obtain the client's agreement to any arrangements proposed.

RIBA Project Manager for a construction project: Form of Appointment (PM/99) April 2004

Under this form of contract, the following functions and responsibilities may be selected from the following list:

Work stages

Feasibility

1   Appraisal: Identification of client's requirements and preparation of studies to enable to proceed and select appropriate procurement method.

2   Strategic brief: Preparation of strategic brief by or on behalf of client. To identify procedures, structure and range of consultants to be employed on the project.

Pre-Construction

1   Outline proposals: Includes development of Project Brief and review of procurement route.

2   Detailed proposals: Completion of Project Brief and application for detailed planning approval.

3   Final proposals: Preparation thereof.

4   Production Information: Preparation of production information to enable tendering, to address any other contractual requirement and apply for statutory approval.

5   Tender documentation: Prepare and collate.

6   Tender action: Identify suitable contractors and evaluate their bids.

Construction

1   Mobilisation: Appoint contractor, provide production information and site access.

2   To practical completion: Administration of contract and provision of further information to contractor.

3   After practical completion: Administration of contract.

The Project Manager's Services are obligatory under this form of contract:

1 Receiving client's requirements and identifying constraints.

2 Conducting feasibility studies/other optional appraisals.

3 Development and maintenance of a project strategy.

4 Advising on selection and appointment of professional skills.

5 Development of management structure and communications environment.

6 Management of development of Strategic Brief into Project Brief.

7 Development, implementation and maintenance of procedures.

8 Preparation and maintenance of a master programme and co-ordination with consultants'/contractors' programmes.

9 Preparation and maintenance of a master cost plan and co-ordination with consultants'/contractors' cost plans.

10 Regulating and reporting to client on performance, cost planning and control and programme and progress.

The following Other Roles are optional:

1 Where appointed as design leader: PM has authority for directing the design process; co-ordinating design; establishing the form and content of design outputs, interfaces and verification procedure; communicating with the client on various design issues.

2 Where appointed as lead consultant: PM has authority in the pre-construction work stages for –

   (i) Co-ordination and review of progress of design work

   (ii) Facilitating communications between client and consultant

   (iii) Advising on need for and scope of services by consultants

   (iv) Advising on procurement methods

   (v) Receiving regular status reports from each consultant

(vi) Developing and managing change control procedures

(vii) Reporting to client where appropriate

3   Where appointed as lead consultant and contract administrator PM has responsibility in the tender and construction stages for -

(i)   Inviting and evaluating tenders, including selection of a contractor and preparation of the building contract

(ii) Administering the contract including review of programme, issuing information and instructions, preparing and certifying valuations of work and collating record information

(iii) Co-ordinating and reviewing the work of consultants and site inspectors including receiving reports, consulting those whose designs may be affected by an instruction, managing change control procedures and providing information to consultants

(iv) Communications between client and consultants

(v)   Reporting to client as appropriate

The following Other Services are optional:

−   Selection of consultants
−   Options appraisal
−   Selection of sites/buildings
−   Outline planning submissions
−   Environmental studies
−   Surveys, inspections or special investigations
−   Accessibility audit
−   Community architecture services
−   Party wall matters
−   2 stage tendering
−   Negotiation of price with contractor
−   Use of energy
−   Value/risk management services
−   Maintenance and operational manuals

- Specially prepared drawings of a building as built
- Special images produced at client's request
- Submissions of plans for approval of landlords, tenants etc
- Applications or negotiations for grants
- Extended handover
- Feedback
- Holding client's money
- Historic buildings and conservation requirements including inspection, listed building consents, grant aided works, historical research and conservation area consents
- Services connected with construction management, financial management, client equipping, surveys and inspections, tenancies
- + any other services that are agreed

The following Special Services may be instructed:
- Exceptional negotiations with planning/other authorities
- Revision of documents to comply with statutory requirements and make general corrections
- Investigations linked to work not done in accordance with building contract
- Assessment of alternative designs/materials
- Ascertainment of contractor's claims
- Services to client linked to any dispute between client and another party
- Activities following damage to buildings, determination of any contract, any party's insolvency, in connection with easements or legal agreements

See *Pozzolanic* (at chapter 2) for extreme and non-standard scope of the project manager's duties.

1.3 THE APPROACH OF THE COURTS

A detailed analysis and comparison of the various standard terms available for appointing a contract administrator is outside the scope of this casebook. This book attempts only to identify those general principles emerging from the case law which concern the duties and rights of those involved in contract administration. The following cases illustrate the importance of looking at each situation on its own facts.

Chesham Properties v Bucknall Austin (1996)

This case involved an analysis of the duties of a number of different professionals on a project: architect, project manager, engineer, quantity surveyor. It was observed that:

> '... the extent of a professional person's duties depends upon the terms and limits of his or her retainer ...'

The question in the case was whether each professional had a duty to advise the employer of deficiencies in a) his own work, and b) the work of the other professionals. Both of these duties were found to be *possible* depending on the terms of engagement and various findings made in respect of the professionals in the case.

London Borough of Merton v Leach (1985)

Per Vinelott J:

> '[Under the JCT Standard Form, 1963 Edition] the architect acts as the servant or agent of the building owner in supplying the contractor with the necessary drawings, instructions, levels and the like and in supervising the progress of the work and in ensuring that it is properly carried out. He will of course normally though not invariably have been responsible for the design of the work ... To the extent that the architect performs these duties the building owner contracts with the contractor that the architect will perform them with reasonable diligence and with reasonable skill and care. The contract also confers on the architect discretionary powers which he must exercise with due regard to the interests of the contractor and the building owner. The building owner does not undertake that the architect will exercise his discretionary powers reasonably; he undertakes that although the architect may be engaged or employed by him he will leave him free to exercise his discretions fairly and without improper interference by him.'

Pride Valley Foods Ltd v Hall & Partners (Contract Management) Ltd (2001)

This case concerned a devastating fire at a bakery in County Durham. In the course of his judgment, HHJ Toulmin QC had to consider the relevance and importance of the expert evidence before him concerning project management, and concluded:

> 'In this case I made observations, both in the course of the interlocutory procedure and at trial, as to the value of expert evidence relating to project management. I expressed the view that what Halls had agreed to do depended on the terms of the contracts with Pride Valley and in particular on the scope of their duties as set out in App 1 to their terms of engagement ...
>
> There is an initial difficulty in accepting expert opinion evidence in relation to the duties of project managers. There is no chartered or professional institution of project managers nor a recognisable profession of project managers. In so far as it may be appropriate to accept expert evidence, the nature of the evidence that might be acceptable will depend on what the project manager has agreed to do. In some cases the project manager will be the architect who will design the project and then, acting as project manager, supervise the contractor and the sub-contractors in carrying out the work. At the other end of the scale the project manager will supervise the work of the contractor and sub-contractors and ensure that the work is carried out in conformity with the design drawings. In these circumstances the project manager will have no design function even to the extent of providing an outline specification. This bears no relation to the function of the architect acting to project manage his project.'

1.4 APPLICATION OF THE *HOUSING GRANTS, CONSTRUCTION AND REGENERATION ACT* 1996

An important consideration for every contract administrator is the effect of the *Housing Grants, Construction and Regeneration Act* 1996, which introduces a series of rules for qualifying 'construction contracts' entered into after 1 May

1998. Such rules are now widely understood and regularly invoked by contractors and employers alike. The following helpful summary of the minimum requirements of a construction contract to which the Act applies appears in *Keating on Construction Contracts* (8th edition) at para. 17-006:

'1   A right to refer disputes to adjudication that will have interim binding effect;

2   An entitlement to periodic payments, with an 'adequate mechanism' for determining what payments become due under the contract;

3   A mechanism for ensuring that unless the appropriate notice is given in time, moneys may not be withheld;

4   A [contractor's] right to suspend performance for non payment;

5   A partial prohibition of 'pay when paid' clauses.'

Section 107 of the Act sets out which contracts will qualify as 'construction contracts': in short, for a contract to be regulated by the same, it must be an agreement either in writing or evidenced by writing for the carrying out of construction operations. Certain contracts such as the delivery of materials to site and contracts with a 'residential occupier' are excluded. For more detail, refer to *Keating on Construction Contracts* (8th edition) at paras. 17-001 to 17-011.

1.5 SUMMARY

- The scope of the contract administrator's duties in relation to construction works will depend primarily on the terms of the specific retainer in question.

- A tribunal may be reluctant to admit expert evidence relating to contract administration and/or project management.

PART 2:
The Functions of a Contract Administrator

2
Project management

At present, as with 'contract administration' there is neither an agreed definition of a 'project manager' nor a recognised professional body of project managers. This is perhaps not surprising, given that project managers themselves often migrate laterally into the position, having acquired experience in other professions. Nevertheless, there is an abundance of case law on the subject, and the courts have had to grapple with practical and procedural problems that the emergent profession has thrown up, particularly in the area of expert evidence.

2.1 THE PROJECT MANAGER

Pozzolanic Lytag Ltd v Bryan Hobson Associates (1999)

The defendant civil and structural engineers were engaged to provide services of consultancy, negotiation of contracts and project management for the claimant in respect of the construction of some storage facilities. A contractor was duly engaged under a form of contract that required it to have adequate insurance for the works being carried out.

The storage facility proved seriously defective. The contractor (which had no assets) was found not to be insured in respect of the loss.

As project manager, it was part of the defendant's responsibilities to ensure that relevant insurance cover was in place in accordance with the contract and it was in breach of that duty.

Palermo Nominees Pty Ltd and Micro Bros Pty Ltd v Broad Construction Service Pty Ltd (1999)

In this reported case from the courts of Western Australia, the claimant was the owner of a hotel and engaged the defendant

17

as a project manager in relation to demolition works and the construction of a new service station and nightclub on the hotel site.

Upon practical completion of the nightclub in October 1994, it became apparent that the premises suffered from unfavourable acoustics and excessive reverberation. The claimant alleged that the defendant should have carried out an independent report into the internal acoustics of nightclub prior to its construction and brought proceedings in which it contended that the defendant was in breach of its express obligation to arrange and coordinate the works to ensure that the claimant's 'requirements and objectives' were achieved to the claimant's reasonable satisfaction.

The court held that, notwithstanding the fact that the defendant had engaged an architect, the expertise involved in ensuring that the internal acoustics of the nightclub were satisfactory for its intended use were beyond those to be expected of an ordinary architect and the defendant was thus in breach of its retainer for failing to procure an independent specialist report.

Royal Brompton NHS Trust v Hammond (2000)

The defendant consulting mechanical and electrical engineers were part of a large team of professional advisors for a hospital development scheme. The work was late and the claimant argued that the defendant (among others) was responsible for the delay and disruption caused.

One of the alleged reasons for the delay and disruption was that the defendant had failed to provide the contractor with co-ordination drawings in sufficient time to carry out the works to programme.

It was held on the terms of the defendant's retainer that it was obliged to use reasonable skill, care and diligence to ensure that the co-ordination drawings were produced in time. This duty was not diluted by any co-ordination obligations which were contained within the building contract.

Rosehaugh Stanhope plc v Redpath Dorman Long Ltd (1990)

A clause in a trade contract purported to give to the construction manager power to make a (temporarily) binding estimate of loss caused by breaches of contract by the trade contractor causing delay. The Court of Appeal found that the clause was ambiguous and, properly construed, did not give the construction manager power to make a binding decision as to the trade contractor's liability. Unless, therefore, liability was admitted or proved or unarguably existed, the construction manager's estimate was not binding and no payment had to be made pursuant to it.

Royal Brompton Hospital NHS Trust v Hammons (2002), (2003)

In this complicated case, the court recognised that project management was (at the time, at least) an 'emergent professional discipline'. However, notwithstanding the fact that very few people train as 'project managers' as their primary profession, and whilst conceding that project management is not 'codified', the court accepted that standards of practices exist which are generally recognised as adequate or inadequate. HHJ Lloyd QC further stated that project management, by its very nature, is about harnessing and coordinating the talents and resources of the other members of the project-specific team; as a result, a project manager's competence is often not dependent on whether a person has managed a particular type of project before.

Costain v Bechtel (2005)

The claimants were a consortium of contractors who collaborated to carry out construction works to refurbish St Pancras station in London as part of the Channel Tunnel Rail Link project. During the course of the works, the rail operations manager called a meeting of Bechtel staff who were involved in the project management of the refurbishment works. The claimants alleged that during this meeting, Bechtel was deliberately instructed to unfairly administer certification of works under the contract, and that the defendants acted in breach of an implied term to act fairly and impartially between employer and contractor (as to which, see *Sutcliffe v Thackrah* (1974)).

The court ruled that whilst in the process of discharging many of its functions under the contract, the project manager may well act solely in the interests of the employer, it would nonetheless be 'most unusual' for a building contract to postulate that every doubt thereunder should be resolved in favour of the employer. However, as the dispute in question was before the court for injunctive relief (as opposed to a final determination), it was not decided whether or not, in these particular circumstances, the project manager owed a duty of impartiality in relation to the works.

John Mowlem & Co plc v Eagle Star Insurance Co Ltd (1992)

This dispute arose out of redevelopment works to a hospital in West London. The claimant, a well-known firm of building contractors, brought proceedings against the developer and architect following the latter's issue of certificates of deduction which entitled the developer to withhold payment to the claimant and the issue of a certificate which terminated its employment. Mowlem was appointed under a management contract which was not in standard form, and alleged that the architect had wrongfully interfered with the performance of the contract and had failed to act independently of the developer.

In refusing to strike out Mowlem's claim, HHJ Loyd QC held that where a contract administrator is appointed to issue certificates fairly and independently in respect of building works, and fails to do so by simply yielding to the wishes of one of the parties (in this case, the developer), then he may be held liable for interfering with the building contract. It seems that in order to ground liability in this way, Mowlem would have to establish that the architect had actual knowledge of the existence of the management contract and intentionally interfered with its performance.

Great Eastern Hotel Co Ltd v John Laing Construction Ltd (2005)

The defendant, John Laing, was employed under a management contract to oversee the procurement process in respect of refurbishment works to the Great Eastern Hotel in London. John Laing's responsibilities under the management contract encompassed the selection, administration and coordination of the works with a multitude of trade contractors. One of the terms of the management contract (specifically, clause 3.4) provided that John Laing was to 'procure that each Trade Contractor complies with all of its obligations under and all the requirements of their respective Trade Contracts'.

The works were substantially delayed and the final construction cost was over £25m more than the claimant had budgeted for. One of the reasons for the overspend was that works were omitted from the scope of individual trade packages and fell to be ordered as variations.

The claimant brought proceedings against John Laing, arguing that its obligation under clause 3.4 was an absolute obligation to take all steps to ensure the trade contractors' compliance with the trade contracts. The court disagreed; John Laing was not a 'guarantor' for the works. HHJ Wilcox held that as John Laing's primary obligation was to carry out its retainer with reasonable skill, care and diligence, the scope of John Laing's obligation under clause 3.4 was that of a professional man carrying out professional services. In any event, John Laing was deemed to be in clear breach of this professional obligation and was held liable both for the claimant's loss of profit as a result of the hotel's late opening, and for the enhanced cost of effecting the omitted works by way of variation instructions as opposed to as part of a trade package.

Scheldebouw BV v St. James Homes (Grosvenor Dock) Ltd (2006)

The claimant was a firm of cladding contractors engaged by the defendant under three separate contracts (the terms of which being substantially the same) for the carrying out of cladding works as part of a waterside development. The defendant appointed Mace Ltd as construction manager for procurement purposes under each of the three contracts.

During the course of the works, the defendant and Mace Ltd mutually agreed that Mace Ltd's appointment was to cease and the defendant sought to appoint itself as construction manager instead. The claimant brought proceedings alleging that the defendant's conduct was repudiatory.

Mr Justice Jackson held that the defendant, as employer, was not entitled to appoint itself as construction manager, as it would undermine the mechanisms of a contract which require a third party to 'hold the balance fairly as between employer and contractor'.

In so reaching his conclusion, the judge found that in the reported cases where the employer acted as certifier of the works, this was pursuant to an express term in the contract permitting the same. Thus, it seems that the concept of an employer carrying out tasks which traditionally fall to contract administrators is not impermissible provided that the parties have agreed to the same.

Mr Justice Jackson reiterated that the duty of the contract administrator to act in a manner which has been referred to interchangeably as impartial, independent, fair and/or honest, boils down to an obligation to use his professional skills and his best endeavours to reach the right decision, as opposed to a decision which favours the interests of the employer.

2.2 SUMMARY

- The contract administrator finds himself in a 'dual' position: whilst he is an agent of the employer, he must act fairly and impartially in managing affairs under a building contract.

- It is unlikely that, in the absence of clear and express words, a contract administrator will be charged with 'guaranteeing' the success of a construction project. However, he will owe to the employer a duty of care to carry out works to a professional standard.

3
Supervision

In large-scale construction projects, a contract administrator may be charged with carrying out some kind of supervisory role in respect of the ongoing building works. There is no hard and fast answer as to the precise degree of supervision which may be required, as this will depend on the terms of the underlying retainer. For example, the RIBA Conditions (PM/99) contain no such duty of supervision. Nevertheless, as the selected cases tend to show, a supervisory duty is not to be underestimated, as failing to carry out any, or any adequate, inspections may have serious consequences for the construction professional.

3.1 SUPERVISORY DUTY

Jameson v Simon (1899)

An architect's duty is to give such supervision as will reasonably enable him to certify that the work of the contractors has been executed according to the contract. This duty is not fulfilled by making occasional visits to the site and ordering the correction of any defects he happens to spot on those visits.

Sandown Hotels Ltd v Phelps (1953)

The architect was engaged to supervise the repainting of a seaside hotel and had wide experience of seaside conditions. The paint began to flake off prematurely because the wood surface had not been properly prepared for the painting. It was found that the architect failed sufficiently to supervise the works, as in the circumstances he should have given particular attention to this aspect of the job.

Sutcliffe v Chippendale & Edmondson (1971)

The architect's duty of supervision under the 1963 edition of the RIBA Standard Form of Building Contract was summarised as being a duty 'to give such periodical supervision and inspection as may be necessary to ensure that the works are being executed in general accordance with the contract'. It was held that:

- constant supervision does not form part of the duties;
- the degree of supervision required must be governed to some extent by his confidence in the contractor (so if something occurs giving the architect reason to doubt the contractor's competence the standard of supervision should be higher);
- the architect is not required to tell the contractor how his work should be done;
- the architect must follow the progress of the work and take steps to see that those works comply with the general requirements of the contract in specification and quality.

East Ham v Bernard Sunley (1996)

The contract provided that the architect's final certificate (issued at the end of the defects liability period) was to be conclusive evidence of the sufficiency of work and materials *save* as regards defects which 'reasonable examination' would not have revealed.

The meaning of 'reasonable examination' was considered. While the architect had a duty throughout the contract to certify satisfactory completion on an interim basis, this clause envisaged an examination at the *end* of the defects liability period. In other words, any defects that would not have been discovered at this stage (even if they may have been discoverable at a previous stage of the contract) were not within the scope of the final certificate and could be the subject of a claim against the contractor.

Department of National Heritage v Steenson Varming Mulcahy (1998)

This dispute concerned a contract for the construction of the British Library in London. The Department of National

Heritage engaged the defendant consultant mechanical and consulting engineer, as well as a cabling contractor and a project manager. Under the terms of his engagement the engineer had a duty to supervise the work of the employer's contractor so as to identify cable damage and required it to be put right, but he had no duty to prevent the contractor doing bad work, which would be akin to the role of a foreman. His duties were limited to taking steps which would discourage bad work and, if possible, discover it after it had been done.

AMF International Ltd v Magnet Bowling Ltd (1968)

In most building projects, an architect is employed directly by the employer and, having no contractual link to the contractor, has no right to instruct him how to carry out the works. It is for the builder to carry out the works as he sees fit and for the architect (acting as the employer's agent) to make sure that the building, when completed, will be properly constructed (citing *Clayton v Woodman* (1962)). The architect therefore had no duty to warn the builder about the flood precautions unless he was asked by the employer to advise on this.

Florida Hotels v Mayo (1965)

The architect's duty to supervise was not discharged by relying (on the basis of past satisfactory performance) on the workmen whose work they were employed to supervise. He was obliged to make reasonable arrangements to remain informed as to the general progress of the work and to be notified as to key elements of that work. Thus, where the work included the pouring of concrete over formwork and reinforcement (which later failed), arrangements should have been made that that work would not be covered up until the architect had inspected it (or had adequate opportunity for its inspection).

Campbell Flour Mills v Ellis & Connery (1914)

The plaintiff milling company engaged the defendant architects to prepare plans and a specification for the construction of a feedmill and to supervise the construction works themselves. It was common ground that the plans, if adhered to, would have resulted in a problem-free building.

However, the architects failed to supervise the contractors adequately or at all, and a defective belt of concrete was deployed in the substructure of the building during construction. The court had no hesitation in finding the architects liable for negligent supervision.

Dabous v Zuliani (1976)

Two prefabricated chimneys were installed by the builder. The architect noticed that the first was installed improperly and warned the builder to correct this. When the second was installed, the same mistake was made by the builder but was covered up before the architect inspected it. The architect made no attempt to make an examination of the second chimney. Because of the faulty installation a fire broke out causing damage.

The court held that since the installation was so critical to safety, and since the architect had already identified a similar fault, the architect was negligent in failing properly to inspect the installation of the second chimney.

Saunders & Collard v Broadstairs (1890)

A finding of 'extraordinary' and 'disgraceful' negligence was made against architects engaged (amongst other things) to supervise construction of a drainage scheme. The fact that the employer also engaged an incompetent clerk of works (on whom the architect relied, knowing he was incompetent) was no defence.

Lee v Lord Bateman (1893)

Where the architect accepted the (wrong) view of the clerk of works as to the sufficiency of certain beams without himself carrying out an inspection, he was negligent if the beams turned out to be insufficient. Reliance on the clerk of works was not a defence.

Leicester Board of Guardians v Trollope (1911)

The employer engaged both an architect (the defendant) and a clerk of works. The clerk of works fraudulently allowed the builder to lay the floor defectively. The architect relied entirely on the clerk of works in this regard and so failed to observe the defect in construction. The architect was negligent and could not rely as a defence on the fact that the employer had engaged a fraudulent clerk of works.

It was observed that the distinction between the clerk of works and the architect was that the clerk of works is expected to deal with matters of detail while the architect is not. However, on the facts the architect had failed to see that an important part of his design was carried out properly.

Kensington & Chelsea & Westminster v Wettern Composites (1984)

The claimant engaged (as independent contractors) the defendant architects and engineers on the project to extend a hospital. It also employed (as its servant) a clerk of works. The ordinary standard of skill and care expected of an architect must be judged with regard to any special circumstances in the case.

Although the clerk of works had been negligent in overlooking certain defects, this did not reduce the architect's liability to use reasonable skill and care to ensure conformity with design as opposed to matters of detail.

However, because the employer was vicariously liable for the contributory negligence of the clerk of works, damages against the architect were reduced by 20 per cent to account for this.

Brown & Brown v Gilbert-Scott (1992)

'Supervision' was not considered to be different from a duty to 'inspect' the works as they progressed (compare, however, the decision in *Consarc Design v Hutch* – see below – in which this case does not appear to have been cited).

The standard of care to be expected of the architect in inspecting the works depends on the circumstances. Relevant factors may include (a) the age and experience of the contractor; and (b) the price being paid for the work (applying *Cotton v Wallis* (1955) (as to which, see chapters 6 and 7 below). In judging the architect's performance, one must look at frequency of visits, the duration of each visit, what the architect did and how the visits fitted into the work being done by the builders.

Alexander Corfield v David Grant (1992)

When considering the question of what was sufficient supervision for the architect to have undertaken, the judge said that it should be asked 'whether it was enough ... The proof of the pudding is in the eating. Was the attention given enough for this particular job'. To the extent that this suggests the architect's duty should be measured by reference to the result achieved, such an interpretation was expressly disavowed by the same judge in *Consarc Design v Hutch* (see below). This case does confirm, however, that the supervision required from time to time will vary depending on the nature of works being carried out. Certain jobs may require exclusive attention, while other stages of the works may need only looking at from time to time (cf. *Brown & Brown* – see above).

Consarc Design v Hutch (2003)

'Inspection' (as required in this contract) was considered by the judge to be a lesser requirement than 'supervision'.

In relation to both inspection and supervision, the architect's duty was said to be one of exercising reasonable skill and care in seeking to achieve a particular result and not of guaranteeing that a particular result will be achieved (cf. *Brown & Brown* –see above).

Clayton v Woodman (1962)

The claimant was a bricklayer working for builders employed to do work on a hospital building. Part of the specified work involved joining an existing tower to a new wall. It was difficult (but possible) to do this safely, and the claimant suggested to the architect engaged by the employer that the specification be changed. The architect refused to do this. The claimant carried out the work in an unsafe manner, the tower collapsed and he was injured. The claim against the architect was dismissed: liability for the claimant's injuries lay with his employers (the builders) alone (cf. *Clay v Crump* – see below).

Clay v Crump (1963)

The defendant architect was employed to supervise a demolition and building operation. The demolition contractors left a wall in an unsafe condition. The architect should have known it was unsafe, but he failed to examine it properly and instructed that it should be left (relying on the demolition contractors). When the building contractors came on site they assumed that the architect considered the wall to be safe. The wall subsequently collapsed, injuring one of the building contractor's employees who brought the claim against (amongst others) the architect.

The architect was found liable to the claimant (distinguishing *Clayton v Woodman* – see above) because he was within the class of person who might be expected to be affected by the architect's negligent breach of duty. The architect knew (or should have known) that the building contractors would not examine the wall closely.

The difference between this case and *Clayton v Woodman* is that here the architect gave a positive instruction which was negligent. In *Clayton v Woodman* the architect simply declined to alter the specification (and was not required to do so).

Oldschool v Gleeson (1976)

On a demolition and building project the builders negligently carried out their works resulting in the collapse of a wall. They admitted liability to the claimant employer and sought an indemnity from the employer's consulting engineer, arguing that the engineer owed a duty of care to the builder as regards (amongst other things) supervision of the works.

The court held that the manner of execution of the works in order to achieve the engineer's design was a matter for the builder. The engineer was not therefore under a duty to draw the builder's attention (for example) to the inadequacy of the shoring to the wall. (The court also observed that even if the engineer were to see a situation developing posing a serious risk of damage to property, the engineer's duty would go no further than to warn the builder to take necessary precautions.)

Imperial College v Norman & Dawbarn (1986)

In considering the standard of competence expected of an ordinarily skilled architect, it is necessary to have regard to the particular circumstances of the case.

Where, therefore, an architect specified the use of external ceramic tiling as a cladding material, a competent architect needed to take particular care in design and supervision of the works because of the known danger of water penetration using this material if improperly installed. However, having regard to prevailing knowledge at the time the architect had not been negligent in recommending the use of this material or in failing to give warnings as to its life expectancy.

Gray v TP Bennett (1987)

The work was for construction of a nursing home. It included a reinforced concrete panel structure fronted by brick cladding which was supposed to be supported by reinforced concrete 'nibs' and wall ties. It was subsequently discovered that 90 per cent of these nibs had been hacked back, leaving the brickwork unsupported.

The judge found that the destruction of the nibs had been deliberately concealed by the builders from the architect, the engineer and the clerk of works.

In the circumstances:

- none of the architect, the engineer or the clerk of works had been negligent in failing to see that the reinforced concrete frame was properly set out or for not detecting the destruction of the nibs; and

- the deliberate wrongdoing of the builders would in any event have broken the chain of causation.

Driver v William Willett (1969)

As a result of a hoist being used in an unsafe manner, the claimant (a labourer) was injured. He sued his employer (the building contractor) and also a firm of consulting safety and inspecting engineers which had been employed by the building contractor to advise it on safety requirements. The consultant engineers had failed to advise the building contractor to discontinue the unsafe use of the hoist which caused the accident. They were therefore liable to the claimant (together with the building contractor) for the injuries suffered (*Clay v Crump* (see above) applied).

Merton LBC v Lowe (1981)

The defendant architects were employed to design and supervise the construction of an indoor swimming pool. The ceiling was to be plastered with a proprietary coating. When cracks appeared in the ceilings of nine different rooms, the architect relied on the contractor applying the coating to repair the cracks. No further investigation was carried out at that stage.

When it was later discovered that the entire ceiling was unsafe and had to be stripped, it was held that the architect was in breach of his professional duty in failing to check the design when it became apparent that there might be a problem with it.

Anglian Water Services Ltd v Crawshaw Robbins Ltd (2001)

The defendant contractor, employed by the claimant on the ICE Conditions (5th edition) to do drilling works, damaged underground gas, water and electricity supplies. The engineer supervising the work was an employee of the claimant. The claimant alleged that as a result of the damage it had become liable to others in respect of the damage and suffered loss.

On a trial of preliminary issues it was found (inter alia) that the engineer owed his supervisory duties under the contract to the employer. Even if he could and should have detected and prevented the accident, this would not excuse a breach of contract by the contractor. (Different considerations would, however, arise if the engineer had negligently given instructions causing loss, damage or injury.)

Victoria University of Manchester v Hugh Wilson (1984)

This case concerned the construction of a university building which was clad in ceramic tiles to be applied to the substructure using an adhesive known as 'Bal-Mix'. The tiles failed due to the subcontractors' misapplication of the Bal-Mix during the 'buttering' process, and remedial works were required which involved cladding the building with bricks tied into the underlying structure.

The court held that if the areas of tiling had been small and the subcontractors had only been on site for a short period, the supervising architects might have been excused for not detecting the subcontractors' failures. However, HHJ Newey QC ruled that given that the areas of tiling were extensive, coupled with the fact that subcontractors were working on site from 1969 to 1972, it should be inferred that the architects did not inspect properly, thus giving the misapplication of the Bal-Mix their 'tacit approval'.

Great Eastern Hotel Co Ltd v Laing (2005)

As set out above in Chapter 2, the defendant was employed under a 'Construction Management Agreement' to manage the procurement and supervision of a hotel refurbishment project. In the event the hotel was late in opening and losses were suffered as a consequence.

The judge referred to construction management as a 'relatively recent' development by which:

> '... the construction manager manages the construction of the project without accepting the principal risks of time and cost, which remain with the client ... [I]t is the obligation of a construction manager to plan, programme and organize the project and the trade contractors who actually carry out the work, so that the client's risks in relation to time and money are minimised'.

The construction manager had the obligations of a professional man performing professional services (as defined by the contract). It was in breach of those obligations and was accordingly liable for the resultant loss of profit.

Tesco Stores Ltd v Norman Hitchcox Partnership (1998)

In 1993 an arson attack on a new shopping development in Maidstone led to a catastrophic fire, causing substantial damage. The defendant architects were sued for inadequately designing the fire retardation methods and/or failing to supervise and properly inspect the building works both during and post construction. The core of the allegation was that the fire would have been less extensive and spread less quickly had adequate design and/or supervision been carried out.

The court held that whilst the defendants could be criticised in respect of their designs, it was not the case that such shortcomings led to the fire spreading more quickly. Further, simply because the architect was empowered to certify practical completion did not impose a duty to carry out a re-examination of the fire retardation methods. Again, the terms of the contract are critical: in this particular case, the architect's obligations under the contract were to design the shell of the building, and did not extend to carrying out inspections prior to certifying practical completion. Absent express words or express instruction, the defendants had no reason to anticipate that their obligations were somehow 'enlarged' to include an inspection duty.

Six Continents Retail Ltd v Carford Catering Ltd (2003)

The respondents (and defendants in the action at first instance) were engaged by the appellants as project managers for the design and installation of kitchen equipment. During the installation process, and contrary to manufacturer's instructions, a rotisserie was mounted on a combustible timber stud wall faced with plywood and tiles.

Following practical completion, problems occurred with the rotisserie as it failed to generate sufficient distribution of heat. Modification work was undertaken, during the course of which some of the tiles became detached from the wall, leaving the rotisserie fixed to the combustible wall beneath without any, or any sufficient, heat shield.

The appellants contended that the respondents owed, and breached, a continuing duty of care to ensure that the rotisserie was installed safely. The respondents denied liability on the basis that they had provided the appellants with a letter over six weeks previously, recommending the installation of a stainless steel plate behind the rotisserie, and that the appellants' failure to act upon such advice broke the chain of causation.

The Court of Appeal held that the respondents were indeed liable, ruling that the respondents' letter was not sufficient so as to constitute a 'warning' and, in any event, even if it was, it operated merely to warn the appellants of an outcome which the respondents themselves should have prevented happening in the first place. Furthermore, the Court of Appeal refused to make any finding of contributory negligence.

George Fischer Holding Ltd v Multi Design Consultants Ltd; George Fischer Holding Ltd v Davis Langdon & Everest (1998)

The defendant was a firm of quantity surveyors engaged by the claimant in respect of a project to build a new warehousing complex for the claimant's business in Coventry. The defendant's duties pursuant to the terms of its retainer were wide-ranging, viz.:

- to obtain and approve design drawings and documentation;
- to carry out the function of 'Employer's Representative' under the building contract;
- to make sufficient visits to the site so as to monitor the contractor's workmanship and progress;
- to check on the conformity of the as-built works to the specification; and
- to report generally on the progress and quality of the works having regard to the building contract.

Soon after completion of the warehouse, serious leaks occurred which resulted from the 'risky' decision to install lap joints on the roofing. It was found that the defendant made no visits whatsoever to view the roof during the periods when the panels were being laid.

The claimant contended that the defendant was in breach of its obligation properly to supervise the works and in issuing a certificate of practical completion in circumstances where the works were clearly not finished.

The defendant denied liability on the following grounds:

- access to the roof was not safe;
- the defective formation of roof seals would not have been detected during an ordinary inspection in any event;
- it was probable that the roofers would simply 'put on a show' to give the impression that roofing was being laid correctly;
- the claimant was putting the defendant under pressure to gain access to the property which would be achieved through the issue of a practical completion certificate.

HHJ Hicks QC rejected all of the above defences, holding that:

- the defendant should have required the contractor to provide safe access to the roof;

- the defendant should have paid 'special attention' to the roofing process due to fact that the 'formation of joints was so obviously crucial';

- further, as the defendant had a responsibility to review the roof designs prior to construction, it was incumbent upon it to exercise the 'closest and most rigorous inspection and supervision of the process' as a result of its 'very risky and inadvisable inclusion of lap joints in such shallow slopes';

- it was part of the necessary skill of a competent inspecting officer to 'detect and make allowances' for workmen who are suspected of 'putting on a show';

- as the defendant lacked the requisite professional training to permit it to properly review the designs, it was under a duty to engage subconsultants in order to discharge its responsibilities;

- it was no defence to the improper issue of a practical completion certificate that the claimant was pressurising the defendant to gain access to the building.

HHJ Hicks QC remarked that a contract administrator may well find himself in a position where he is facing demands for access to the property from the client and pressure from the contractor for the issue of a certificate. In such circumstances, where (as in this case) the contract administrator is contract-bound to report generally on the progress and quality of the works, he is expected carefully to advise his client of the merits and demerits of the contractor's demands for the issue of a certificate and of the strengths and weaknesses of the client's bargaining position in order to reach a commercial compromise. Further, if any such compromise is stuck, the contract administrator will be responsible for making a record of the agreed terms and to seek confirmation from all relevant parties of the accuracy of such a record.

3.2 SUMMARY

- As always, the first port of call when establishing a contract administrator's supervisory role (if any) is to look at the terms of the retainer.

- The degree and/or extent of supervision required will depend on the nature of the works and the particular facts of the case.

- If in doubt, a contract administrator should seek advice from appropriate subconsultants and keep the employer aware of developments at all times.

- Reliance on third parties and/or other members of the project team may not afford a defence to an employer's allegation of negligent supervision.

4
Instructions, information, variations and waivers

During the course of a construction project, the contract administrator may find himself under intense pressure to make quick decisions to ensure the smooth and timely progress of building works. As the middleman between contractor and employer, he will inevitably find himself fielding questions and answering requests of various parties on site on a daily basis. Problems occur when instructions provided by a contract administrator lead to additional and/or varied work being carried out under the contract. Unsurprisingly, the contractor will seek payment for any extras, and the employer may well be very unwilling to release more funds (especially if the contract administrator does not have a contractual power to order variations). Alternatively, a contractor may seek to rely on the fact that he was simply following the contract administrator's instructions as a defence to an allegation of defective workmanship. The following cases provide an illustration of how the courts have dealt with such scenarios.

4.1 INSTRUCTIONS AND INFORMATION

Neodox Ltd v Borough of Swinton and Pendlebury (1958)

It was an implied term of the contract that the employers (by their engineer) would provide details and other instructions necessary for the execution of the works from time to time during the course of the contract within a time reasonable in all the circumstances.

Royal Brompton NHS Trust v Hammond (2000)

The defendant consulting mechanical and electrical engineers were part of a large team of professional advisors on a large hospital development scheme. The work was late and the claimant argued that the defendant (among others) was responsible for the delay and disruption caused.

One of the alleged reasons for the delay and disruption was that the defendant had failed to provide the contractor with co-ordination drawings in sufficient time to carry out the works to programme.

It was held on the terms of the defendant's retainer that it was obliged to use reasonable skill, care and diligence to ensure that the co-ordination drawings were produced in time. This duty was not diluted by any co-ordination obligations which were contained within the building contract.

4.2 VARIATIONS: INCREASING OR DECREASING THE CONTRACTOR'S SCOPE OF WORKS

R v Peto (1826)

In the absence of an express power given to a surveyor to vary the works, it was no answer to a claim of defective work that the contractor had followed the surveyor's instructions. There was no implied power for a surveyor to vary the works.

Sharpe v San Paulo Railway (1873)

Pursuant to a contract under seal, building contractors agreed to construct a railway for a fixed price and to accept payment therefor following the issue of a certificate by the project engineer. There were express terms of the contract that the certificate as a condition precedent to payment, and the engineer's valuation of the works in that certificate was 'final and conclusive on both parties (i.e. the contractors and the defendant railway company), without any appeal'.

During the course of the works, the engineer instructed the contractors to carry out construction of the railway in accordance with new plans, which occasioned the execution of earthworks greatly in excess of the quantities originally envisaged under the contract. The contractors objected, and in response, the engineer verbally assured that considerable savings would be made on other areas of the railway so as to keep costs to the original budget.

The Court of Appeal ruled that even though the amount of works carried out was understated in the engineer's certificate, there was no claim against the defendant for further payment. The engineer had no power to vary the contract; if the contractors thought that certain works were not within the contract, then they were not bound to do them. In the circumstances, extra works should have been carried out under a separate contract with the defendants. The fact that the engineer had made verbal promises to the contractors was irrelevant, as no such promises had come from the defendant company.

Stockport MBC v O'Reilly (1978)

O'Reilly was a building contractor who was engaged by a local authority to construct a series of houses and related works. O'Reilly brought arbitration proceedings against the council employer to recover monies which it alleged were due under the contract. As the works progressed, the architect gave O'Reilly instructions which it was not empowered to do so under the terms of the contract.

The court robustly held that an architect has no authority to vary the contract, and any acts in excess of the Authority would not saddle the employer with liability to pay further sums to a contractor. If the parties are faced with such a situation, they can either agree to the same (thus varying the contract) or may protest against them and ignore them.

Carlton Contractors v Bexley Corporation (1962)

Prior to the issue of a formal contract, the claimant building contractors realised that there were discrepancies between the drawings and bills of quantities for the works produced by the defendant authority. At a pre-contract meeting, the defendant's borough surveyor (who was the architect and surveyor for the works) met with the claimant and agreed a series of variations to the contract which were recorded into a document. The contract was subsequently signed, but failed to incorporate the above variations.

The court, in finding for the claimant, held that the borough surveyor was acting within the scope of his authority in negotiating the terms of the contract at the pre-contract meeting, and could, in the circumstances, make an agreement to vary the terms of the contract which was binding on both parties. Ungoed-Thomas J further held that the fact that the variations were included within a document which was not under seal (as opposed to the contract, which was sealed) was irrelevant. The intentions of the authority did not need to be in a sealed document in order to be properly recorded.

Sir Lindsay Parkinson & Co. Ltd v Commissioners of Works (1949)

The claimant contractors were engaged by the defendants to construct an ordnance factory for a lump sum of £3.5m. The commissioners had an express power to vary the contract in order to modify the extent and/or character of the works and it was the duty of the contractors to comply with the architect's instructions in this regard.

During the course of the works, delays occurred for which the contractor was not responsible and an extension of time was granted. The employer ordered that the works be accelerated to meet the original deadline and undertook to pay further sums to the contractor as a result. As it happened, the original bills of quantities anticipated a further £500,000 worth of works in any event.

However, as the accelerated works progressed, further variations and alterations were ordered.

The court held that by accelerating the works, the parties entered into a varied contract, into which a term would be implied that if the work was to be materially varied in excess of 500,000l, any works carried out over and above that sum were to be valued on a quantum meruit basis.

This demonstrates the need for the architect or contract administrator to exercise due caution when issuing variations: if the variation departs so far from the original scope of works that it cannot fairly be regarded as part of the original bargain, it will constitute a separate contract, which may not be subject to the same terms.

Davy Offshore v Emerald Field Contracting (1991)

There was no implied term obliging the employer (no architect was engaged) to issue a variation order where to do so would be 'fair'. In passing, the judge commented that this function was to be distinguished from that of an architect 'holding the balance' between the parties where a requirement to act fairly would be implied.

Kimberley v Dick (1871)

The employer engaged the architect who contracted with the claimant builder as agent for the employer. The architect in his contract with the employer undertook that the works would be carried out for no more than £15,000 but the builder was never told of this. The building contract price was £13,690. The architect had however power to order extras and did so.

The court held that the builder was entitled to the full cost of such extras and was not bound by the limit agreed between the employer and architect.

AMEC Building Contracts Ltd v Cadmus Investments Co. Ltd (1996), (1997)

The claimant was employed to carry out construction works to build a shopping centre, part of which concerned the creation of a food court. The fitting out of the food court was covered by certain provisional sums in the original contract sum. During the course of the works, and pursuant to an architect's written instruction, the fitting out of the food court was omitted from the scope of the claimant's contract works and was instead let to another contractor. The claimant sought to recover its loss of profit in respect of the food court works.

It was common ground between the parties that the architect was permitted to omit provisional sums or parts thereof if the works to which they relate are not in fact required. The contract expressly empowered the architect, in his sole discretion, to withdraw any work from provisional sums for whatever reason, if he considered it to be in the best interests of the project or the employer to do so.

However, the claimant was entitled to compensation (namely loss of profit) following an arbitrary withdrawal of work in order to award the same to a third party. It is noteworthy that the Recorder arrived at this conclusion with some reservation, apparently drawing on the arbitrator's finding of fact (which the court could not disturb) that omitting work only to award the same to another contractor was commonly considered bad practice and contrary to 'good faith' in the construction industry.

4.3   SUMMARY

- A contract administrator should ensure that he is aware of the scope of his powers under the contract in question. Ordering variations without authority can have very serious repercussions indeed.

- In general terms, a contract administrator will not have authority to increase or decrease the scope of works unless this is expressly set out in the contract.

- It appears that an express power to omit provisional items from a contractor's scope of works must be exercised in 'good faith'.

5
Extensions of time, liquidated damages, and loss and expense

The 'dual' role of the contract administrator as an agent of the employer and as middleman between employer and contractor during a construction project can come under intense pressure when it comes to regulating the time in which construction activities are required to be carried out or when dealing with delays to the works. Often the contract administrator will be under pressure from the employer to secure completion of the works on time (or even ahead of schedule) and to refrain from sanctioning any extensions to the completion date. Conversely, the contractor will rely on the contract administrator to act fairly so that it does not incur the burden of liquidated damages. It may be that the award of an extension of time and/or liquidated damages is contingent upon written notice from either the contractor, the employer or the contract administrator himself.

5.1 EXTENSIONS OF TIME

Sindall Ltd v Solland (2001)

The defendant developer engaged the claimant contractors pursuant to IFC 1984 terms and conditions to renovate a property known as Lombard House in Mayfair, London. The works did not run smoothly; following an award of an extension of time (which was later extended following adjudication proceedings), the contract administrator purported to terminate the claimant's employment pursuant to clause 7.2.1 of the contract on the grounds that it was not proceeding diligently with the works. The claimant contractors commenced adjudication proceedings for a declaration that the termination was unlawful and for an award of a further extension of time.

In enforcing the adjudicator's award, the court held that when evaluating a claim for an extension of time, a contract administrator should consider all matters which might give rise to a valid claim, not solely those identified and put forward by the contractor. Such considerations would be all the more important where the employer is seeking to determine the contractor's employment by relying on an alleged failure to proceed diligently with the works.

Amalgamated Building Contractors Ltd v Waltham Holy Cross UDC (1952)

The claimants were engaged to construct houses pursuant to a standard form of contract issued by RIBA and the National Federation of Building Trades Employers. Building works fell into substantial delay, largely as a result of the contractors' difficulty in procuring labour and materials, which was a contractual ground for an extension of time, which was duly applied for.

The architect did not consider the contractor's claim until after completion of the building works. The contractors claimed that the architect's contractual power to make a 'fair and reasonable extension of time for completion of the works' meant that the architect must exercise this discretion timeously, i.e. so as to give the contractors a date at which they could aim at to complete the works. In other words, the contractors claimed that the power to issue an extension of time could not be exercised retrospectively.

Lord Justice Denning (as he then was) rejected this contention, holding that there was nothing wrong in awarding a retrospective extension of time. It was always open to the contractor to seek relief through arbitration if it was dissatisfied at the architect's dilatory conduct in considering a claim for an extension of time and/or issuing a certificate.

Walter Lawrence v Commercial Union Properties (1984)

This case concerned the 1963 JCT standard form of contract and the contractor's claim under the same for an extension of time as a result of 'exceptionally inclement weather'. The principles established in the case are of equal effect to the JCT 1980 form of contract and IFC 1984 form of contract.

HHJ Hawser QC held that the effect of the 'exceptionally inclement weather' on the progress of the works is to be assessed at the time when the works are *actually* carried out, not when they were supposed to be carried out under the construction programme. In other words, when considering a claim for an extension of time arising out of bad weather, the contract administrator (in this case the architect) was not entitled to dismiss the claim simply by stating that the affected works should have been carried out earlier.

The JCT 2005 standard form of contract refers to 'adverse weather conditions' as opposed to 'exceptionally inclement weather'. It is thought that the same reasoning applies (see *Keating on JCT Contracts* at 1.1–103).

Balfour Beatty Ltd v Chestermount Properties Ltd (1993)

Under the extension of time provisions in the JCT standard form (1980 edition) the architect had power to grant an extension of time in respect of variations ordered during a period where the contractor was already in culpable delay. Such variations did not therefore constitute acts of prevention whose effect was to set time at large.

The effect of such variations (and therefore the extension of time) should be considered as the extent to which the period of contract time available for completion ought to be extended or reduced, having regard to the incidence of the variations (or other relevant events) (the 'net' approach). The architect was *not* therefore to assess the length of time required to carry out the variation works and refix the completion date at the end of such period starting from the date of the variation instruction (the 'gross' approach).

John Barker Ltd v London Portman Hotels Ltd (1996)

This dispute concerned refurbishment works to a London hotel under the JCT standard form of contract (1980 edition). The contract provided for sectional completion dates for portions of the work, on a floor-by-floor basis. The parties fell out over the contractor's entitlement for an extension of time which, under the contract, fell to the architect to determine fairly and reasonably.

The court held that in deliberating over the award of an extension of time, the architect was under an implied obligation to act lawfully, rationally and fairly. This would involve carrying out a logical analysis in a methodical way of the impact that the relevant matters would have on the claimant's construction programme. Further, should the parties be conducting their affairs under a standard form contract with quantities, the architect should pay close attention to the content of the bills before arriving at his decision. It is not necessary to prove bad faith on the part of the architect.

If an extension of time decision is held to be invalid, then the matter might be put back before the architect in question to redetermine the relevant facts and make a fresh award. However, on the facts of the case, this was not practically possible given the absence of contemporaneous notes and the passage of time, as well as being undesirable from a costs perspective. In order to get around this problem, the court ruled that the underlying contractual machinery had broken down to such an extent that empowered the court can step in to determine what is a fair and reasonable extension of time. The court hinted that if, on the facts, an architect's award was only invalid in a 'discrete' respect that the matter could be referred afresh for a revised determination.

City Inn Ltd v Shepherd Construction Ltd (2003)

In this case, the Inner House of the Court of Session in Scotland considered a clause making the contractor's provision of notice of delay a condition precedent to any entitlement to an extension of time. If the contractor fails to give such notice, then the result is drastic: the contractor forfeits any such entitlement. Contrary to what one might perhaps expect, there are no clever legal arguments which can circumvent such a provision. The court expressly rejected the submission that the clause in question was penal.

5.1.1 Summary

- Some standard form contracts will assist the contract administrator in determining whether or not a contractor's claim for an extension of time ought to be granted, whether by expressly recognising delay events or otherwise.

- When considering a contractor's claim for an extension of time, a contract administrator may well be obliged to consider all circumstances which contribute towards delay, not merely those put forward by the contractor.

5.2 PROBLEMATIC OR 'CONCURRENT' DELAY CLAIMS

Sometimes the contract administrator will have to consider a contractor's application for an extension of time in circumstances where more than one factor was responsible for project delays. It goes without saying that each claim or group of claims in respect of delay must be examined on its own facts. It often transpires that a particular event is not a cause of critical delay at all, or not in fact concurrent. Nevertheless, one of the roles of the contract administrator may well be to consider the comparative potency of causal events.

Heskell v Continental Express (1995)

In circumstances where there are several delay 'events', and if a particular delay event is one of the causes cooperating and of equal efficiency in causing loss to the contractor, an extension of time should be granted as long as the event for which the employer is responsible is an 'effective' cause of the same.

Successive editors of *Keating on Building Contracts* have suggested that the 'dominant cause approach' is the correct approach to apply when choosing between competing causes. This requires an architect to choose between two competing causes of delay, with the 'dominant' cause being operative.

Henry Boot Construction (UK) Ltd v Malmaison Hotel (Manchester) Ltd (1999)

This case considered the problems concerning repetition delay faced by an architect under JCT Standard Form of Building Contract (1980 edition), but is noteworthy for its common-sense approach to 'concurrent' causes of delay under a construction contract. When delay manifests itself during the course of building works, the contractor is to submit a written notice outlining the causes of delay and their anticipated effect on the overall construction programme. It then falls to the architect to study the notice, and, if satisfied that events are 'relevant events', fairly and reasonably refix the completion date.

The court held that it was a question of fact whether a relevant event (such as exceptionally inclement weather) caused or is likely to cause delay to the works, in circumstances where there is a concurrent cause of delay which is not a relevant event (such as a shortage of labour). The architect is *not* precluded from considering such other causes of delay when determining whether a relevant event is likely to cause to delay to the works beyond completion.

Laing Management (Scotland) Ltd v John Doyle Construction Ltd (2004)

John Doyle were engaged as works contractors by management contractors (Laing) to carry out certain work packages for the construction of new headquarters for Scottish Widows. The contract was an amended form of Scottish Works Contract (1988). John Doyle sought an extension of time of 22 weeks, made a substantial claim for loss and expense (over £4m) and a claim upon the final account. With regard to the loss and expense claim, this was calculated utilising a comparison between pre-contract estimates and actual costs, i.e. a 'global claim'.

Laing accepted that, in principle, it was permissible to advance such a claim if it were impossible to trace the causal nexus between each individual event and each item of loss, although the burden of showing this was upon John Doyle. Laing maintained, however, that such an approach was only permissible if John Doyle was *not itself* responsible for any increased costs and Laing was responsible for *all* the causal factors that contributed to the increased costs.

Laing further contended that since, on the facts, it could be readily demonstrated that an element of the delay was not the fault of Laing, one of the essential factors for a global claim to succeed was absent. Accordingly, Laing contended that John Doyle's claim should not be allowed to proceed to trial.

The Inner House held:

1   For a loss and expense claim under a construction contract to succeed, the contractor must normally plead and prove individual causal links between each alleged breach or claim event and each particular item of loss and expense.

2   *If* it is impossible to separate out the consequences of each of the alleged claim events *and* the contractor is able to demonstrate that all of the events on which he relies are in law the responsibility of the employer, it is not necessary for him to demonstrate causal links between individual events and particular heads of loss.

3   However, if it is proved that a *significant* cause of the (cumulative) delay alleged was a matter for which the employer is *not* responsible a global claim must necessarily fail.

4   If an event or events for which the employer is not responsible cannot be categorised as significant the claim may not fail.

In such cases, an apportionment exercise may be feasible, although this may produce a somewhat rough and ready approach.

Great Eastern Hotel Company Limited v John Laing Construction (2005)

The defendants advanced the argument that the claimant's case ought to fail as it was unable to demonstrate the causal nexus between major breaches of contract and particular loss and damage. HHJ David Wilcox ruled (at para. 328):

'I am satisfied that the Trade Contractor accounts are global claims, and if such a claim is to succeed, GEH must eliminate from the causes of the loss and expense element all matters which are not the responsibility of Laing. That requirement is mitigated in this case, because it was not possible to identify a causal link between particular events for which Laing was responsible, and the individual items of loss. Such an analysis was approved by the Court of Session Inner House in *John Doyle Construction Limited v Laing Management (Scotland) Limited* ... I am satisfied ... that the dominant cause of Trade Contractor delay was in fact the delay to the project caused by Laing's proven breaches.'

HHJ Wilcox then carried out an exercise of apportionment in accordance with expert opinion. However, pursuing global delay claims is still somewhat of a risky enterprise for the contractor. The onus of proving that loss has been suffered remains firmly the responsibility of the contractor.

London Borough of Merton v Stanley Hugh Leach Ltd (1985)

Under clause 23 of the JCT standard form (1963 edition, although the judge's discussion remains at least partially relevant for later editions). It was held that: the architect owed a duty to both the contractor and the employer in assessing extension of time and it was not a condition precedent to the grant of an extension of time that the contractor should have given written notice of the cause of delay. However, it was submitted that in any event the contractor must not benefit from his breach by receiving a greater extension than he would have received had the architect upon notice at the proper time been able to avoid or reduce the delay by some instructions or reasonable requirement.

JCT 2005 Standard Building Contract with Quantities (SBC/Q)

Despite changes made to the above 1963 edition by the JCT 1980 Standard Form of Building Contract (and carried into the 2005 form), it is thought by the editors of *Keating on JCT Contracts* (at 1.1-084) that the principles in *Merton v Leach* remain valid at least in relation to the grant of an extension of time after practical completion.

5.2.1 Summary

- It may be that the contractor's issue of a written notice is a condition precedent to the granting of an extension of time. Care should be taken to scrutinise the relevant contractual provisions.

- Concurrent delaying events are problematic; however the most recent authorities suggest that the courts may be willing to take a more liberal approach to dealing with complicated delay claims.

5.3 CONTRACT ADMINISTRATORS AND THE PROBLEM OF FLOAT

'Float' is an additional period allowed for in a contractor's program beyond that which is needed for any activity before the next activity on the critical path.

Disputes over the 'float' arise in circumstances where a delay on the part of the employer 'eats into' the time set aside by the contractor as the float. Contractors will argue that they have a right to an extension of time to make up for the 'employer event', whereas the employer will maintain that a completion date is a completion date, and the concept of a float is not something with which they concern themselves.

5.3.1 Position under JCT standard form contracts

The mechanics of JCT have curious consequences in respect of 'float', which stem from the fact that the JCT standard forms do not expressly recognise the concept.

Thus, where initial delays are caused to a project on account of variations or 'employer events' such as problems with accessing the site or late supply of design information, such matters will not be causative of delay to the completion date as they are absorbed by the 'float'.

Such circumstances can be somewhat unfair to contractors where 'employer' delays use up the float, meaning that subsequent 'contractor' delays mean that no extension of time is granted and trigger the payment of liquidated damages. In other words, a contractor will be deprived of the benefit of its contingency plan (i.e. the float) through no fault of its own. Obviously, the order in which 'contractor' and 'employer' delaying events occur is impossible to predict and is outwith the control of the contractor.

The Royal Brompton Hospital NHS Trust v Frederick Alexander Hammond and others (2002)

His (Honour Judge) Humphrey Lloyd was of the opinion that in situations such as that described above, an appropriate extension, not exceeding the float, should be given:

> 'The architect should in such circumstances inform the contractor that, if thereafter events occur for which an extension of time cannot be granted, and if, as a result, the contractor would be liable for liquidated damages then an appropriate extension, not exceeding the float, would be given. In that way the purposes of the clause can be met: the date for completion is always known; the position on liquidated damages is clear; yet the contractor is not deprived permanently of 'its' float ... In practice however architects are not normally concerned about these points and may reasonably take the view that, unless the float is obvious, its existence need not be discovered.'

Whilst only a first instance judgment, it seems to suggest that the float is owned by the project, whilst possibly also building in a level of protection for the forward-thinking contractor.

5.3.2 Position under NEC3

What has been discussed so far has been in relation to JCT 2005. The concept of a float has different implications for NEC3 due to the differing nature of this type of contract.

In an NEC3 contract, the program is revised periodically (generally monthly) with the consequence that projected completion dates for each stage are continually being assessed and reassessed. The hope is that, as a result, float is much less likely to be a point of contention due to the fact that it will be continually revised and float (providing, of course, that it is properly disclosed) will be protected when changes are made to the completion date.

5.3.3 Summary

- At present, although it is possible that under JCT forms of contract, it would seem that an architect does not need to preserve the 'float' for the benefit of the contractor. The position is different under NEC3.

- In practical terms, the issue of 'float' will only become an issue vis-à-vis extensions of time in circumstances where an activity subject to any period of 'float' is deemed to be on the critical path.

- Any potential 'injustice' over ownership of float may be avoided by inserting an express contractual clause stipulating that in any extension of time award, the contractor's float must be taken into consideration and preserved. This, of course, involves a level of transparency, as it will oblige contractors to disclose any float which may be disguised in a complicated construction programme.

5.4 LIQUIDATED DAMAGES

Peak v McKinney (1970)

Where any part of the delay to the works had been caused by the employer in circumstances where no extension of time was due, there could be no liability for liquidated damages.

The editors of *Keating on JCT Contracts* (at 1.1-113) suggest that a contract administrator may be under a duty to advise the employer of this principle of law if it becomes apparent that it might apply during the course of construction works. Should the employer withhold payment on erroneous grounds that liquidated damages are payable, then the contractor has an express right to terminate the contract.

Bramall & Ogden v Sheffield CC (1983)

The dispute between the claimant contractor and the defendant concerned the defendant's right to deduct liquidated damages and the extensions of time granted pursuant to a JCT standard form (1963 edition) contract for the construction of 123 dwellings. Clause 16(e) provided for a reduced sum to be payable after taking partial possession while the appendix provided for the award of liquidated damages 'at the rate of £20 per week for each uncompleted dwelling'. The date for completion was stated as 6 December 1976 and the final practical completion certificate awarded for each section of buildings taken over was given on 20 September 1978. No formal sectional completion agreement was entered into. The defendant kept back £26,150 in liquidated damages.

The court, on appeal from an arbitrator's decision, found that in the absence of any provision for sectional completion the defendant was not entitled to claim or deduct liquidated damages as provided in the appendix.

It was held that the contract did not provide for sectional completion, that the defendant had taken possession under clause 16(e), but that clause 16(e) was inconsistent with the liquidated damages appendix so was unenforceable. Thus a provision for liquidated damages will be construed against the maker of the provision seeking to rely on the same and, if inconsistent with the contract provision to which it relates, will not be enforced.

Bell & Son (Paddington) Ltd v CBF Residential Care and Housing Association (1989)

The claimant contractor entered into a contract with the defendant for the construction of an extension to a building. The agreement was in the JCT standard form of building contract (1980 Private Edition) with quantities, and liquidated damages for non-completion were stated to be at the rate of £700 per week. Under clause 24, the architect was required to issue a certificate if the contractor failed to complete the works by the completion date, upon which the employer could inform the contractor in writing of its intention to subtract liquidated damages. A series of extensions of time were duly granted, for one of which a certificate and notice were issued, but after fixing a completion date of 20 May 1986, no further certificate was given until the final certificate on 25 April 1988. The defendant withheld £4,900 in liquidated damages, for which amount the claimant applied for summary judgment.

The court, finding for the claimant, held that the correct construction of the contract required a certificate to be issued when a contractor failed to complete the works by the completion date and that a notice was superseded along with the certificate to which it applied. A certificate and notice were conditions precedent to the award of liquidated damages and in this instance neither had been given.

Philips Hong Kong Ltd v AG (1993)

The claimant was one of seven contractors with the Government of Hong Kong for the design, supply , installation and supervision of a processor-based supervisory system for the approach roads and twin tube tunnels of a major highway. The appendix provided for liquidated damages to be payable in the event that certain 'key dates' were missed, and for failing to complete the whole of the works within the time specified. The amount of liquidated damages payable for failure to meet a key date varied according to which key date was missed. The claimant sought a declaration that the relevant clause was unenforceable, succeeding at first instance. Eventually the Privy Council dismissed the claimant's case, stating that:

1   The test for deciding whether a liquidated damages clause is penal is to consider whether or not it is a genuine pre-estimate of what the loss is likely to be.

2   A liquidated damages clause will not be penal simply because there may be situations in which the clause's application might result in recovery over and above actual loss suffered.

3   An employer, in pre-estimating liquidated damages, should carefully consider the types of losses which might arise and factor these into any formula it uses.

4   A minimum payment provision is not penal if it can be reasonably assumed that a delay in completion will inevitably continue to incur expenses irrespective of the scale of work.

JF Finnegan Ltd v Community HA Ltd (1995)

The claimant was a contractor employed by the defendant to build 18 flats under a JCT standard form of building contract 1980 private edition with quantities. A dispute arose over the deduction of liquidated damages, which the defendant did having issued a certificate and given written notice in a form which the court at first instance found to be inadequate.

The Court of Appeal, finding for the defendant, held that:

1 written notice by the employer is a condition precedent to the deduction of liquidated damages under the contract;

2 written notice can be given at the same time as the deduction is made;

3 written notice has to make clear that liquidated damages are being deducted and the extent of those liquidated damages. There is no need to explain the period for which a deduction is made.

5.4.1 JCT 2005

Under clauses 2.31 and 2.32 of the JCT 2005 standard form of building contract, the contract administrator is obliged to issue a certificate of non-completion regardless of whether the employer intends to impose liquidated damages.

5.5 LOSS AND EXPENSE

LB of Merton v Leach (1985)

The defendants were the main contractors for the claimant in relation to the construction of 287 dwellings. The defendants were appointed under the JCT standard form (1963 edition, 1971 revision). A number of disputes arose and were referred to arbitration, to be subsequently appealed by the claimant pursuant to the *Arbitration Act* 1979.

Amongst other issues, the court considered whether the terms of the contract permitted the contractor to recover direct loss and expense when it was not possible to say with any certainty how much loss and expense could be attributed to a particular event.

It was concluded that where an application is made for reimbursement of direct loss and expense attributable to more than one head of claim, and at the time when the loss or expense comes to be ascertained, it is impossible to attach a specific amount to each head of claim, the contract administrator should:

1 ascertain the global loss attributable to the various causes;

2 disregard any loss or expense which would have been recoverable if the claim had been made under one head of claim in isolation and would not have been recoverable under the other head of claim in isolation.

Therefore, so long as the contractor had not himself caused the confusion through unreasonable delay, he was not to be unfairly deprived of an intended benefit.

Croudace Construction Ltd v LB of Lambeth (1986)

The claimant was contracted by the defendant to erect a number of flats and shop units under the terms of the JCT local authorities edition with quantities (1963 edition, 1977 revision). A few months into the project, a mains electrical cable was discovered, causing a delay while the London Electricity Board provided for its diversion. Practical completion was achieved some nine months after the contract completion date, whereupon the claimant submitted a claim for loss and expense, albeit in the absence of an architect's final certificate. The defendant refused to acknowledge the claim and summary judgment was entered for the claimant in the sum of an interim payment of £100,000.

Dismissing the appeal, the Court of Appeal held that the defendant's refusal to acknowledge the claim, including the failure to appoint a successor architect, had meant that the claimant was unable to ascertain its claim and as such amounted to a breach of contract by the defendant. Although a claim was not possible under the contract in the absence of an architect's certificate, the claimant was entitled to damages if it could be shown that it had suffered some damage. The burden fell on the defendant employer to establish that there were no matters in respect of which the claimant might claim under the contract; if it could not, it necessarily followed that the claimant had suffered some damage as a result of the failure to ascertain sums due.

H Fairweather & Co. Ltd v LB of Wandsworth (1987)

The claimant was employed to carry out the construction of 478 dwellings in accordance with the JCT local authorities edition with quantities (1963 edition, 1973 revision). A variety of issues came before an arbitrator, one of which was whether an extension of 81 weeks awarded by the architect could be reallocated to allow for the recovery of direct loss and expense under the contract. Finding that the extension did not carry with it any right to claim direct loss and expense, the arbitrator decided that the extension was granted in respect of the dominant reason for delay.

The question of whether the arbitrator had been correct in law was appealed. The court found that the 'dominant reason' approach adopted by the arbitrator was incorrect, but that the arbitrator had in any case misinterpreted the contract and was obliged to reconsider this part of the award anyway.

GMTC Tools & Equipment Ltd v Yuasa Warwick Machinery Ltd (1994)

The claimant, manufacturers of rotary cutters used in the engineering industry, purchased an electronic precision lathe from the defendant which proved seriously defective in that it either failed to work at all or did so intermittently. The claimant brought proceedings for breach of contract, initially claiming for a number of management hours and a flat rate of £25 for each hour that the lathe did not work.

The court found for the claimant on liability but refused to allow it to re-amend its claim in relation to quantum to reflect its buying in of finished rotary cutters and its inability to seek new business.

The Court of Appeal was unimpressed by this refusal, holding that although a trial judge was required to control proceedings a party should not dictate the case that a party should advance, especially when that case was unrepresentative of the true basis of the party's claim. It was therefore allowed on the further grounds that the defendant would not be prejudiced by the amendment.

Alfred McAlpine Homes North Ltd v Property & Land Contractors Ltd (1995)

The claimant entered into a contract with the defendant for the building of an estate of 22 houses under the JCT form of building contract (1980 edition). Shortly after the works were commenced, the claimant issued an instruction to postpone the works, giving rise to a claim by the defendant for direct loss and expense under the contract. The calculation and amount of the claim were referred to an arbitrator whose decision was subsequently appealed.

One issue which fell for consideration was whether overheads and profit constituted direct loss and/or expense within the meaning of the contract, the judge holding that it was not necessary to differentiate between whether a head of claim represented 'loss' or 'expense'. As to the award of overheads and profit, the judge found that although the use of a formula might provide a broad assessment of the likely amount, it could only be valid if the necessary assumptions were appropriate and the parties concurred that such an approach was efficient and economical. Therefore findings of fact were crucial and should, so far as possible, be based on actual loss and expenditure.

AMEC Building Contracts Ltd v Cadmus Investments (1997)

The claimant was a contractor for the construction of a retail centre in Rochdale under a contract that was novated to the defendant. Following practical completion, a variety of matters were brought before an arbitrator and subsequently appealed to the High Court. Amongst other issues to fall for consideration, the court was asked to decide on the extent of proof required by a claimant to demonstrate that a contractor had been unable to recover its proportion of head office overheads due to the employer's default, and on whether the arbitrator had been correct to reject the claimant's unparticularised global approach to its claim for disruption.

On the first issue, the court found that the arbitrator's approach in applying a formula to those parts of the overheads which he was satisfied fell to be awarded was correct. As for the global approach adopted by the arbitrator, it was held that the arbitrator was right to insist on as much detail as possible in the setting out of the claim, but that a court was able to assess damages on an unspecific basis in appropriate circumstances.

How Engineering Services v Lindner Ceilings Partitions plc (1999)

The claimant was subcontracted to the defendant for the installation of a ceiling as part of the redevelopment of

Cannon Street Station. The defendant's works were delayed and disrupted to the extent that an arbitrator awarded loss and expense in the defendant's favour. The claimant appealed, alleging that the arbitrator had erred in his approach to the quantification of the claim because he had accepted a series of assessments that lacked the necessary precision.

In considering *Alfred McAlpine Homes North Ltd v Property & Land Contractors Ltd* (1995), the court found that this case did not say that there is no room for the exercise of judgment in the process of ascertainment and that when assessing loss and expense the tribunal should resort to the use of judgment only where the facts are insufficiently clear.

6
Valuation, certification and termination

As we have seen, a contract administrator is often charged with managing a variety of duties during the course of a construction project, the precise portfolio of work being determined by the conditions of his or her retainer. However, at the heart of the contract is the movement of money: who pays, how much, when and to whom?

It will be in rare circumstances indeed that a contract administrator has nothing to do with cashflow under a building contract. He may be responsible for authorising payments due to the contractor, normally by way of certification. Such certification may require a degree of quality control or inspection. Further, it may fall to the contract administrator to declare that the works are complete, to arrange the handover and/or commissioning of the same, and to manage and maintain the contract during any defects liability period. The following cases consider the differing responsibilities and liabilities of contract administrators as regards valuation and certification.

6.1   FINAL AND CONCLUSIVE CERTIFICATES

Many standard forms of contract provide for a final certificate which is binding and/or conclusive as to certain matters arising under the contract. Obviously the extent to which the certificate may be binding and/or conclusive will depend on the precise words of the agreement in question. It is certainly the case that a binding certificate can have very drastic consequences, both in terms of liability and evidential matters, and may also affect a party's right to bring contribution proceedings.

East Ham v Bernard Sunley (1966)

An architect's final certificate under the RIBA 1950 standard form of contract was conclusive as to the sufficiency of work and materials and was not subject to review by the arbitrator.

P&M Kaye Ltd v Hosier & Dickinson (1972)

This case concerned a final certificate under the 1963 JCT standard form of building contract. A majority of the House of Lords held that the effect of the same was conclusive in proceedings brought either before or after its issue.

HW Nevill Sunblest v William Press (1981)

In this case, the court held that the wording of the 1963 JCT standard form was not conclusive in respect of any consequential loss suffered by the employer in the period between practical completion and the issue of a final certificate.

Colbart v Kumar (1992)

The claimant was a contractor engaged by the defendant under a JCT IFC form of contract (1984 edition) to carry out refurbishment works, who brought proceedings to recover non-payment of sums due pursuant to a final certificate issued by the architect. Clause 4.7 of the contract provided that a final certificate was 'conclusive ... that the quality of materials or the standard of workmanship is, where the proviso to clause 1.1 applies, to the reasonable satisfaction of the Architect' except to the extent that proceedings had been commenced either before its issue or 21 days thereafter.

Clause 1.1 provided that the contractor:

> '... shall carry out and complete the Works in accordance with the Contract Documents: provided that where and to the extent that approval of the quality of materials or of the standards of workmanship is a matter for the opinion of the Architect ... such quality and standards shall be to the reasonable satisfaction of the Architect'.

The claimant contended that clause 4.7 bound the parties and prevented the court from going behind the same. The defendant alleged that the final certificate was conclusive in limited circumstances only, namely where the parties had expressly stipulated in the contract that certain matters had to be carried out to the reasonable satisfaction of the architect. The judge sided with the claimant, holding that more explicit wording would be required to justify a more restrictive construction.

Darlington BC v Wiltshier (1993)

This case concerned clause 30(7)(a) of the JCT 1963 standard form of contract (1977 revision), which provided that the effect of a final certificates was '(i) conclusive evidence that where the quality of materials or standards of workmanship are to be to the reasonable satisfaction of the architect the same are to his satisfaction'. The issue before the court was whether such a final certificate would prevent a party from claiming in respect of any defects in the works.

In distinguishing *Colbart v Kumar*, HHJ Newey QC held that the final certificate applied only to materials and workmanship which were expressly stipulated under the contract to be to the architect's reasonable satisfaction, and to none other.

Cotton v Wallis (1955)

In this controversial case, the claimant architect brought proceedings against the defendant employer for non-payment of professional fees. The employer counterclaimed for the cost of remedying defects which had emerged following the defendant's issue of a final certificate to the contractor under a standard form RIBA contract. Building work was to be done under the contract 'to the reasonable satisfaction of the architect'. It was found that the work contained defects (in the words of the trial judge, it had been 'scamped'). Further, both parties accepted that the construction cost was particularly low.

The Court of Appeal held that, in the circumstances, the architect was not negligent in certifying the works as complete, irrespective of the existence of defective works, as he was permitted to a limited degree of tolerance on account of the low price. This was the case even though the contract bills required that the workmanship and materials were to be of the 'best of their respective kinds'.

Lord Justice Denning (as he then was) dissented from the majority view, holding that it did not matter that the price was a low one; it is the builder's obligation to see that his contract is properly carried out.

It is submitted that this particular case should be treated with caution. The editors of *Keating on Building Contracts* (8th edition, at para. 19-045) suggest that it is not a binding authority as regards disputes between employer and contractor. At the very least, a contract administrator should only look to the price of the works as a last resort, and only if such a course of action does not militate against the express terms of the contract.

Crown Estate v Mowlem (1994)

The decision of the Court of Appeal concerning clause 30.9.1 of the JCT standard form of contract (1980 edition) generated considerable controversy in the industry and triggered the issue of amendment to the JCT form in the 1998 edition (and its equivalent in the 2005 suite). Under that particular contract, the issue of a final certificate was 'conclusive evidence that where the quality of materials or the standard of workmanship are to be to the reasonable satisfaction of the Architect, the same are to such satisfaction'. It was decided that the conclusive effect of the certificate was binding as regards workmanship and materials to *all* materials and workmanship where approval of such matters was inherently something for the opinion of the architect.

Beaufort Developments (NI) Limited v Gilbert-Ash NI Limited (1998)

The House of Lords noted that it was possible that a provision making any certificate 'conclusive' could potentially cause injustice. For example, such a certificate might be given when the knowledge of an architect in respect of the state of the works was incomplete. However, the courts must give effect to the terms of the contract agreed upon between the parties. On the facts, no final certificate had been issued. As a matter of law, under the contract in question, neither interim certificates nor the certificate of practical completion were 'conclusive'.

Matthew Hall Ortech v Tarmac Roadstone (1998)

For the first time, the court was asked to consider the effect of a final certificate under clause 38.5 of the I Chem E form of contract 1981 edition (also known as the 'Red Book') in relation to building works for the construction of a process plant. It was held that the effect of the same was conclusive evidence that all work was completed in accordance with the contract, and that it was legitimate to use the Red Book Guide Notes as an aid to construction.

Oxford University Fixed Assets v Architects Design (1999)

This dispute arose out of building works in Oxford undertaken pursuant to a JCT standard form of contract (1980 edition). The defendant architect issued a final certificate to the contractor following completion of the building works. It later transpired that blockwork walls were in fact defective in that they suffered from widespread cracking. The claimant employer commenced proceedings against the architect for breach of its contractual duty of care.

On deciding two preliminary issues of law, HHJ Humphrey Lloyd held that:

- the architect's issue of a final certificate was tantamount to a discharge of the contractor's liability under the contract; the work was either not defective at the time of its issue, or, if it had once been defective, it had been put right;

- it was not open to an architect to claim a contribution from the contractor: such contribution proceedings would constitute a 'rank injustice'.

In other words, the effect of the final certificate under the particular version of the JCT contract in question (With Contractor's Design) operated as an evidential bar, precluding an employer from being able to prove the facts necessary to ground liability against a contractor.

LB of Barking v Terrapin Construction (2000)

The agreement of the final account and the final statement under clause 30.8.1 of the 1981 JCT WCD was conclusive evidence as to the contractor's compliance with the contract, in respect of both patent and latent defects and compliance with statutory requirements concerning materials and workmanship. However, the clause was not wide enough so as to cover the contractor's responsibility for design.

6.2 POSITION UNDER THE JCT 2005 STANDARD FORM OF BUILDING CONTRACT

Although to the best of the authors' knowledge at the time of writing there are no reported cases in which the mechanisms of the JCT 2005 suite of contracts have been considered by the courts, it is worth setting out the position concerning the conclusivity of a final certificate under clause 1.10 of the JCT 2005 standard form of building contract.

'Effect of final certificate

1.10 1. Except as provided in clauses 1.10.2, 1.10.3 and 1.10.4 (and save in respect of fraud), the Final Certificate shall have effect in any proceedings under or arising out of or in connection with this Contract (whether by adjudication, arbitration or legal proceedings) as:

1 conclusive evidence that where and to the extent that any of the particular qualities of any materials or goods or any particular standard of an item of workmanship was described expressly in the Contract drawings of the Contract Bills, or in any instruction issued by the Architect/Contract Administrator under these Conditions or in any drawings or documents issued by the Architect/Contract Administrator under any of clauses 2.9 to 2.12 to be for the approval of the Architect/Contract Administrator, the particular quality or standard was to the reasonable satisfaction of the Architect/Contract Administrator, but the Final Certificate shall not be conclusive evidence that they or any other materials or goods or workmanship comply with any other requirement or term of this Contract;

2 conclusive evidence that any necessary effect has been given to all the terms of this Contract which require that an amount be added to or deducted from the Contract Sum or that an adjustment be made to the Contract Sum, save where there has been any

accidental inclusion or exclusion of any work, materials, goods or figure in any computation or any arithmetical error in any computation, in which even the Final Certificate shall have effect as conclusive evidence as to all other computations;

3 conclusive evidence that all and only such extensions of time, if any, as are due under clause 2.28 have been given; and

4 conclusive evidence that the reimbursement of direct loss and/or expense, if any, to the Contractor pursuant to clause 4.23 is in final settlement of all and any claims which the Contractor has or may have arising out of the occurrence of any of the Relevant Matters, whether such claim be for breach of contract, duty of care, statutory duty or otherwise.'

As with any contract, it goes without saying that it is very important to study the relevant provisions carefully. This is all the more crucial under JCT 2005, as the final certificate is conclusive in some respects, but not others. Further, its conclusive effect can be limited or even extinguished entirely.

6.3 CHALLENGING THE CERTIFICATE

As we have seen, when a certificate is legitimately 'conclusive' it can have very onerous consequences for an employer if it transpires that defects which should have been picked up by the contract administrator have been overlooked. Where the contractual term relied on is unambiguous, clear and has been properly executed, then an employer cannot look to a tribunal to rescue him from the consequences of a binding and conclusive final certificate. Despite this, there are circumstances in which the court may find that a certificate can be attacked. These are considered below.

6.3.1 Issue of certificate exceeds the architect's jurisdiction

Generally, an architect's decision will not be conclusive upon matters that are not within his jurisdiction. In most circumstances, these will include breaches of contract by the employer, matters arising under a new and independent contract, and where the certificate is given after the expiry of the contractual time-limit set for the giving of the certificate.

6.3.2 Issue of certificate not compliant with contractual terms

A certificate will not be conclusive if it is not made in accordance with the contract. The certificate must be in the correct form, as specified within the contract. The decision to give the certificate must be based upon the architect's own decision. As we have seen, when deciding whether to issue a certificate, the architect must, insofar as is possible, act independently, honestly and fairly.

Cantrell v Wright & Fuller (2004)

In this case, which concerned the construction of an old people's home pursuant to JCT standard form of contract (1980 edition), HHJ Thornton QC held that a document relied upon by the respondent was not a final certificate under the contract as it was issued too early. On the facts of the case, the architect had not completed the exercise of computing the contract price. The court noted that whilst it might be permissible to relax the timescales set out under the JCT forms, this would not obviate the requirement to comply with conditions precedent in order to issue a valid certificate thereunder. It seems that minor departures from a strict application of the relevant contractual conditions may be possible provided that no party is misled.

Clemence v Clarke (1880)

Whilst an architect can obtain advice and assistance from other construction professionals, if he is empowered under the contract to certify then such a certification must be his and his alone. In other words, a wholesale delegation of certification powers is not permissible.

Kensington & Chelsea Area Health Authority v Wettern Composites and others (1984)

In an action against architects and consulting engineers concerning damage sustained as a result of defectively fixed stone mullions, the architects were found to have failed to do all they ought to have done in the supervision of the erection of the extension to Westminster Hospital. The architects had failed to take any action after receiving a clear letter of warning from the engineers about the fixing of the stones. For their part, the engineers satisfied their obligations by drawing the architects' attention to their concerns about the stability of the fixings.

The plaintiff employer had also employed a clerk of works to co-ordinate the construction project. The judge described his duties as being the 'eyes and ears' of the architects, with a responsibility to keep them informed of what was happening on site. The clerk of works was under the architects' direction and control in carrying out his inspection duties. Notwithstanding that, the architects were not vicariously liable for the negligence of the clerk of works, because he was employed by the employer and acted 'solely as the inspector of the employer'. Accordingly, the plaintiff was held to be vicariously liable for the defaults of the clerk of works in failing to spot the defect.

In judging the respective degrees of responsibility between the architects' negligence and that of the clerk of works, the judge held that the latter's default, whilst more than minimal, was much less than that of the architects. Accordingly, the plaintiffs were entitled to recover 80 per cent of the damages sustained.

RB Burden v Swansea Corp (1957)

Under an express clause of the RIBA standard form, the appellant contractors were empowered to terminate the contract in the event that the employer had interfered with or obstructed the issue of a certificate. On the facts, the project quantity surveyor had improperly valued works carried out under the contract and failed to inform either the respondent or the project architect, who went on to issue a certificate in the sum of the improper valuation. The appellants purported to terminate their employment under the contract. It was held that although the valuation was improper, the certificate nevertheless stood, and on the facts the appellant's termination was invalid as no interference with the certification process had taken place.

It seems that the making of a mere mistake will not be sufficient to invalidate a certificate. In such circumstances, the employer can pursue relief against the architect himself (see *Campbell v Edwards* (1976) and *Sutcliffe v Thackrah* (1974)). However, a certificate would not be binding if the architect had strayed substantially from his original instructions.

6.3.3 Disqualification of certifier

A certificate will have no effect if an architect is later disqualified by reason of his conduct when giving the certificate. This could be because he fails to act with professional independence, or if his actions are dishonest, biased or fraudulent.

Kemp v Rose (1858)

The defendant entered into a contract with the claimant contractors for the rebuilding of the Leiston parish church. Prior to the execution of the building contract, the defendant instructed an architect to prepare plans for the rebuilding works at a cost not exceeding 2500l. The architect prepared bills of particulars for the works, against which the claimant prepared an estimate.

The building contract contained an express provision empowering the architect to order variations and request payment for the same. Upon completion of the works, the claimants made a claim for additional payments for works over and above those included in the estimate. The architect refused to allow the payment of the additional sums. The court held that the claimant was entitled to payment; as the architect had 'nearly unbounded' powers under the contract, if there was a circumstance which was tending to bias his judgment and which was unknown to one of the contracting parties, any decision made by him cannot be absolutely binding upon that contracting party.

Kimberley v Dick (1871)

This case is considered at 4.2 above. The claimant contractor entered into a contract with the defendant employer to carry out the construction of a mansion house to the satisfaction of the project architect for a fixed sum. The architect was empowered to grant variations and omissions to the works, and that 'all questions touching the matters relating to this contract shall be left to the sole determination or award of the said architect' ('the arbitration clause'). Prior to the execution of the building contract, the employer had agreed with the project architect that the cost of the works was not to exceed £15,000.

Substantial variations were altered and the contractor sought recovery of additional payments in respect of the same from the employer. The contractor was not aware of the existence of the contract between the employer and the architect.

The court held that the arbitration clause did not extend so as to give the architect the power of acting as judge in matters of difference between himself and the contractor: such jurisdiction was limited to differences or disputes between the employer and the contractor. The contractor could not be bound by an undertaking that he would abide by any decision of the architect in circumstances where he was ignorant of the contract between the employer and the architect. It was the employer's responsibility to inform the contractor of the contract subsisting between himself and the architect in order to make the £15,000 cap effective. As in *Kemp v Rose*, the architect was disqualified to certify matters under the contract as a result of his failure to disclose his contract with the employer.

Brodie v Cardiff Corp (1919)

Where the engineer had power to order that certain works were extras and (wrongly) failed to do so, that decision could be challenged in arbitration, notwithstanding the absence of such an order.

Sutcliffe v Chippendale & Edmondson (1971) *and* Sutcliffe v Thackrah (1974)

The House of Lords held that an architect, charged with issuing interim certificates under a standard form of building contract (in this case, the RIBA form) will not be immune from liability in negligence to his employer. On the facts, the architect had ignored certain defects and thus negligently over-certified sums due to the contractor under interim certificates. The contractor was later ejected from site and became insolvent.

An architect may also be bound to notify the project quantity surveyor of any defective work so that the same could be excluded from the appropriate valuation.

In general terms, a building owner can expect his architect to administer the contract and supervise the work (provided, of course, that supervision forms part of his retainer) to ensure, as far as is reasonably possible, that the quality of the work matches up to the standard contemplated. Whilst a detailed investigation at interim stage may be impracticable, the court held that 'more than a glance round was to be expected'.

6.3.4 Effect of arbitration clause

A contractual arbitration clause may affect the binding and conclusive nature of the certificate. Such a clause may show that the certificate was not intended to be binding on the parties or permit a review of the merits of the certificate. See *Beaufort Developments (NI) Limited v Gilbert-Ash Limited* (1999) discussed above.

6.4 EMPLOYER'S CLAIM AGAINST THE ARCHITECT

Rogers v James (1891)

The final certificate issued by the architect was binding as to the existence of defects as between the employer and the contractor and did not protect the architect in an action for negligent supervision of the work.

Merton LBC v Lowe (1981)

Where the architect negligently issued the final certificate of completion so that the employer was deprived of a remedy against the contractor for defective work, the value of recovery against the architect was the value of the remedial works that the employer was prevented from claiming against the contractor.

Wessex RHA v HLM Design (1995)

The defendant architects, engaged in relation to construction works at a hospital in Bournemouth, were sued by the claimant employer for over-certifying the value of works carried out by the subcontractor. The defendant denied liability on the grounds that an employer under a JCT contract had no independent cause of action against an architect, as the appropriate relief should be sought from the contractor in arbitration proceedings.

HHJ Fox-Andrews QC rejected the defendant's arguments, holding that the employer was entitled to sue either the contractor or the architect or both.

6.5 ISSUE OF WITHHOLDING NOTICES

Where a contract is regulated by the *Housing Grants, Construction and Regeneration Act* 1996 (see 1.4 above), an employer/main contractor may not withhold payment of sums due under the contract to a contractor/subcontractor (respectively) without the issue of an effective notice of intention to withhold payment. This provision is enshrined in section 111 of the Act. Contract administrators may well be asked by the employer to issue such notices on the employer's behalf or to advise on their contents. Careful consideration must be given to the requirements of section 111 which is set out below.

'111 – Notice of intention to withhold payment

1   A party to a construction contract may not withhold payment after the final date for payment of a sum due under the contract unless he has given an effective notice of intention to withhold payment.

The notice mentioned in section 110(2) may suffice as a notice of intention to withhold payment if it complies with the requirements of this section.

2   To be effective a notice must specify –

(a)   the amount proposed to be withheld and the ground for withholding payment; or

(b)   if there is more than one ground, each ground and the amount attributable to it, and must be given not later than the prescribed period before the final date for payment.

3   The parties are free to agree what the prescribed period is to be.

In the absence of such agreement, the period shall be that provided by the Scheme for Construction Contracts.

4   Where an effective notice of intention to withhold payment is given, but on the matter being referred to adjudication it is decided that the whole or part of the amount should be paid, the decision shall be construed as requiring payment not later than –

(a) seven days from the date of the decision, or

(b) the date which apart from the notice would have been the final date for payment,

whichever is the later.'

Strathmore Building Services Ltd v Colin Scott Greig (2001)

A withholding notice must be in writing, and service of the same cannot be effected before an application for payment is received.

Rupert Morgan Building Services v David Jervis (2004)

Defences of set off or abatement (whether on the grounds of defects or delay or otherwise) will not succeed in the absence of a withholding notice, irrespective of the merits of such substantive defences. It is the sum in the certificate which defines the sum due, not the actual work done. The Court of Appeal affirmed that the purpose of section 111 was to preserve cashflow between the parties on a construction project.

6.6 TERMINATION

Terminating a contractor's employment is possibly the most drastic action that a contract administrator may be obliged to take during the course of a construction project. Most standard form contracts have express procedures to be followed in order to make such a termination lawful and effective. In such circumstances, there really is no substitute for reading the contract.

West Faulkner Associates v Newham LBC (1992)

The appellant was a firm of architects who had been sued by the defendant council for failing to issue a contractual notice of termination under a JCT 1963 standard form of contract. Pursuant to clause 25(1)(b) of the same, the employer could terminate the contractor's employment if the contractor failed to 'proceed regularly and diligently with the works'.

Serious delays to refurbishment works occurred on site and, although the council communicated its opinion that the contractor's conduct was such that a notice under clause 25(1)(b) should be issued by the architect, the architect refused to do so. On appeal, the architect argued that for a notice to be issued, the contractor had to be in default *both* by failing to proceed regularly *and* by failing to proceed diligently. It was common ground that the contractor was proceeding diligently.

The Court of Appeal dismissed the architect's appeal, holding that no reasonably competent architect could have arrived at such an interpretation of clause 25(1)(b). Further, their Lordships ruled that unless the architect's construction of a contractual clause is plainly correct, the architect is under a duty to seek legal advice and/or to advise the employer that such advice be sought.

6.7 SUMMARY

- Extreme care must be taken to study, understand and operate the relevant contractual provisions in respect of valuation, certification and termination.

- The consequences of improper certification or operation of termination provisions are drastic. If a certificate is issued negligently, then the employer may find himself without a remedy as against the contractor, and will look to come after the architect for damages. The consequences of an improper or unlawful termination are even more serious;

should this occur, the employer may well find himself in repudiatory breach of the contract in question.

- The authorities make it clear that if in doubt, the contract administrator should seek legal advice or advise the employer to do so.

7
Notification of defects and duty to warn

The specific duties owed by a contract administrator to third parties and other members of the project team are discussed in greater detail in Part 3. However, the duty to identify defects and warn of potential or actual problems during the course of a project is dealt with in this chapter. Efficient project teams and intelligent use of technological advances can certainly reduce the possibility of defects occurring in buildings, but while there is scope for human error there is also scope for defects. If problems manifest themselves during the course of building works, the contract administrator may be under a duty to warn the employer of the existence of the same (if, of course, this is not already an express condition of his retainer).

7.1 DUTY TO WARN

East Ham v Bernard Sunley (1996)

The contract provided that the architect's final certificate (issued at the end of the defects liability period) was to be conclusive evidence of the sufficiency of work and materials, *save* as regards defects which 'reasonable examination' would not have revealed.

The meaning of 'reasonable examination' was considered. While the architect had a duty throughout the contract to certify satisfactory completion on an interim basis, this clause envisaged an examination at the *end* of the defects liability period. In other words, any defects that would not have been discovered at this stage (even if they may have been discoverable at a previous stage of the contract) were not within the scope of the final certificate could be the subject of a claim against the contractor.

William Tomkinson v St Michael in the Hamlet (1990)

The contract (JCT Minor Works, 1980 edition) provided for notice of defects appearing within three months of practical completion to be given by the architect to the contractor.

The defects complained of were notified orally by the architect *prior* to practical completion and remedied by others. The employer was nevertheless entitled to the cost of engaging others to remedy defects appearing prior to practical completion (although recovery was limited to the cost that would have been incurred by contractor).

Cotton v Wallis (1955)

Building work was to be done under the contract 'to the reasonable satisfaction of the architect'. It was found that the work contained defects (in the words of the trial judge, it had been 'scamped'). The fact that the contract was for a low price was a relevant factor in determining whether the architect had been negligent in passing the work as being to 'his reasonable satisfaction'. He was entitled in such circumstances to apply a lower standard.

(See also 6.1.)

Eames London Estates Ltd v North Hertfordshire DC and others (1981)

The third defendant, Mr Hyde, was an architect operating from business premises in Hitchin, Hertfordshire. In 1964, Mr Hyde prepared a design for the development of land adjacent to a railway line and partially comprised of landfill. The foundations were negligently designed and the building suffered serious subsidence as the natural consolidation of the fill began to let down the surface.

The official referee found that it was no defence for an architect faced with an allegation of negligence to contend that he had ascertained what was sufficient in terms of loading to get around the local authority. On the facts, the architect failed to take any boring readings and, critically, put aside a query over sufficiency of loading and foundation depth when it was raised on the spot during construction. The official referee quoted from and approved an extract from the written expert report:

> 'I consider it normal practice for an architect to draw his client's attention to the need for ground conditions to be investigated. Also, that the client be advised of the possible need for a qualified structural engineer to be employed to carry out a detailed site investigation, if the architect was uncertain in any way of the type and bearing capacity of the ground.'

Victoria University of Manchester v Hugh Wilson (1984)

The claimant engaged the defendant architects to design a major development known as the Precinct Centre, which was a cutting-edge construction project involving a reinforced concrete structure clad partly in brick and partly in ceramic tiles. The architects in question had never used ceramic tiles externally before, and sought advice from specialist subconsultants. The tiles proved problematic from the outset and many fell off as a result of weathering and inadequate fixing. Eventually the claimant undertook remedial works to remedy the problems through the erection of brick cladding tied into the structure.

HHJ Newey QC held that whilst nothing was wrong in principle with using a relatively untried system of cladding, an architect will nonetheless be under a duty to warn the employer of potential risks and dangers emanating from the decision to adopt a new method of construction.

Convent Hospital Ltd v Eberlin (1988)

The defendants were a firm of architects who were sued by the claimant employers for failing to procure a performance bond for 10 per cent of the contract sum from the contractor. The contractor went into receivership during the course of construction works to extend a hospital in Nottingham. The architects joined the contractor as a third party to the proceedings, claiming that its director had misrepresented the true position vis-à-vis securing the requisite performance bond.

The court found that whilst the director had made fraudulent misrepresentations stating that the bond was being dealt with by the contractors' insurance brokers and that it would be provided imminently, this was not enough for the architect to claim a contribution from the contractor, as the misrepresentation did not induce the architect to allow and/or advise the employers to enter into the building contract.

Plant Construction plc v Clive Adams Associates (2000)

A subcontractor had inadequately propped a roof during the course of some works with the result that the roof collapsed. The inadequate propping was done to the order of the ultimate employer's engineer.

The fact that the separate consulting structural engineers and the subcontractor's site agent both considered the propping to be inadequate (and said so at the time) did not negative the implied duty that existed for the subcontractor to warn of the danger which it perceived existed. Whether such an implied duty existed depended on the facts of each case.

Aurum Investments Ltd v Avonforce Ltd (2001)

The defendants were engaged to carry out excavation works prior to constructing a basement and garage to a residential property in London. The defendants duly instructed structural engineers to provide advice and engaged specialist underpinning subcontractors to carry out underpinning works. Some two months after the completion of the underpinning works, the defendants commenced excavation works to create the basement, but failed to provide any lateral support to the underpinning, causing it to collapse.

Proceedings were brought against the defendant contractors by the owner of the property, who sought to pass liability onto the underpinning contractors, alleging that they were under a duty to warn the defendants that adequate lateral support to the underpinning was required prior to commencing excavation works adjacent to the same.

The court reviewed the case law on the subject and made the following conclusions:

- If works carried out by a contractor are, by their very nature, obviously dangerous, then a contractor might be under a duty to warn those instructing him that the works are dangerous. Such a duty would arise irrespective of whether those instructing that contractor had procured professional advice.

- If the contractor has no knowledge of the subsequent works to be carried out once his works are complete, then a duty to warn will not arise if the contractor has no reason to believe that the subsequent works will be carried out unsafely and/or negligently.

- It is reasonable for a contractor, in such circumstances, to assume that subsequent works will be carried out safely and with reasonable skill and care.

- Whether a duty to warn will arise is fact sensitive and must satisfy the test of 'reasonableness'.

Pride Valley Foods Ltd v Hall & Partners (Contract Management) Ltd (2001)

In this case, the defendant project managers failed to provide adequate advice and warnings to the claimant as to fire risks and precautions during the building of a purpose-built factory between 1993 and 1995. The building was ravaged by fire in 1995. However, despite the provision of any adequate warning to the claimant, the judge at first instance ruled that the defendant nonetheless escaped liability by establishing that the claimant would not have accepted such a warning in any event as a result of budgetary concerns.

This particular case was remitted to the Technology and Construction Court by the Court of Appeal and, as far as the authors are aware, is currently adjourned.

7.2 SUMMARY

- If the works in question involve the incorporation of new techniques or construction methods, or if their nature is dangerous, the contract administrator is likely to be under a duty to warn the employer of any potential risks which might arise as a result.

- That the employer has procured his own professional advice does not in itself obviate the need for the contract administrator to issue such warnings.

8
Procurement

Part of a contract administrator's duties may be to advise on suitable contractors and/or materials for the project in question. Questions may arise as to whether a contract administrator is liable to the employer for the selection of materials which turn out to be unsuitable, or for suggesting a contractor who transpires to have little or no relevant experience to carry out the works.

Procurement for public works, services or supply contracts (such as those undertaken by local/regional authorities or the state) is subject to European legislation and is outside the scope of this book (for an introduction, see chapter 14 of *Keating on Construction Contracts* (8th edition)).

8.1 SPECIFICATION OF MATERIALS

George Hawkins v Chrysler UK (1986)

These proceedings arose out of a personal injury sustained by the claimant following a fall in communal showers installed in the first defendant's foundry. It emerged that the type of tiling used for the works was particularly slippery. The third party was a firm of engineers who were responsible for preparing the design and specification of the shower room. The engineers had made prudent enquiries prior to putting together the specification, including the investigation of RIBA project sheets, trade brochures, and consultations with a specialist flooring firm. On the facts, they were not found to have been negligent.

Richard Roberts v Douglas Smith Stimson (1988)

The defendant architects designed an effluent tank for the claimant's dyeworks, relying on a quotation from the second defendants (ECC) for the installation of a specialist resin lining. The architects had no knowledge of such specialist linings, but nevertheless approved ECC's quotation and the claimant duly entered into a contract with ECC.

The lining failed. The court held that the architects were liable in negligence and/or for breach of contract for failing to adequately investigate ECC's proposed lining. Part of their role was to be aware of and collect information in relation to new materials. If they were unable to advise on the lining, they should have informed the claimant of this and advised the claimant to seek different advice.

8.2 PROCUREMENT OF CONTRACTORS

Valerie Pratt v George J Hill (1987)

The claimant was the owner of a bungalow who brought proceedings against an architect who, prior to the commencement of construction works, had warranted that two particular firms of builders were 'very reliable'. In reliance on this statement, the claimant entered into a contract with one of them. The builders turned out, in the words of the one of the appeal judges, to have 'done almost everything wrong'. The architect was held liable in damages as a result of his negligent misrepresentation.

Equitable Debenture Assets Corp. Ltd v William Moss Group Ltd (1984)

The defendants were appointed as architects in respect of the construction of an office block. Specialist subcontractors (Alpine) negligently designed the curtain walling, and admitted liability to the claimant developer, before going into liquidation.

The court held that in failing to make proper enquiries about Alpine or asking specialist curtain wall consultants to so do, the defendant was negligent in selecting Alpine to carry out design works. Further, the defendant failed to properly involve the curtain wall consultants when revised designs were received from Alpine prior to their acceptance by the claimant.

Great Eastern Hotel Co. Ltd v Laing (2005)

A construction manager employed under a Construction Management Agreement had as one of his responsibilities to 'scope' the trade contractor packages to ensure they were workable and complete. The construction manager failed to do this, with the result that some works had to be carried out as variations to the works. As this was less economical than carrying them out as part of a competitively tendered trade package, the construction manager was liable for the enhanced cost.

Tyrer v District Auditor of Monmouthshire (1973)

The appellant was a quantity surveyor employed by Monmouth County Council. During the period of his employment, considerable building works took place and a particular building firm secured a number of contracts from the local authority. It transpired that the firm in question had received substantial overpayments as a result of the appellant's approval of excessive quantities and prices in some of the contracts. The contractor subsequently went into liquidation.

The court held that the quantity surveyor was under a duty to ensure that rates which were excessively high were not accepted, even though the appellant was under considerable pressure to carry through the contracts to completion. He was held liable for the overspend.

8.3   OBTAINING QUOTATIONS AND TENDERS

Sika Contracts v Gill & Closeglen Properties (1978)

The first defendant was an engineer who had invited the claimant contractor to supply a quotation for repair works at a property owned by the second defendant. The engineer subsequently accepted the quotation, but neglected to inform the contractor that he was acting as an agent of the second defendant.

The court held that the engineer had contracted personally with the contractor and was responsible for payment.

Partridge v Morris (1995)

The defendant architect was engaged by the claimant, a homeowner, in respect of renovation works at the claimant's property. The defendant recommended a firm of contractors who failed to complete the contract works. As a result, the claimant was obliged to appoint third party contractors to finish off the job at an increased cost.

The court held that an architect's duty to advise on tenders extended to advising on the merits and financial acceptability of each tender. These were matters on which the claimant required advice, especially as there were no other members on the project team. The court also drew support for this analysis from considering the RIBA *Architect's Job Book* , which states that upon return of tenders, an architect should 'discreetly check' the financial status of the relevant building firms.

Hutchinson v Harris (1978)

This dispute arose out of architectural services carried out in relation to building works in Islington, London. The architect was engaged under the RIBA conditions of appointment and failed to procure competitive tenders for the project.

On the facts, it was found that only one tender was obtained and that the architect could not remember why alternative tenders were not sought. However, the claimant was not able to adduce evidence to prove its loss and, in the circumstances, the award of damages was merely nominal.

Scrivener v Pask (1965)

The claimant was a builder who had tendered for the building of the defendant's house based upon quantities and tender documents warranted as accurate by the defendant's architect. It turned out that the quantities were incorrect and the claimant spent much more than he anticipated in his tender.

The court held that there was no evidence that the architect had acted as the defendant's agent, and the defendant had not guaranteed the accuracy of the bill of quantities. In the circumstances, the builder was bound by his tender price and could not recover the overspend from the defendant employer.

8.4 SUMMARY

- A contract administrator should be very careful when obtaining quotations. In some circumstances he might find himself personally liable for the cost of the building works if a quotation is accepted without proper authority of the employer.

- If in doubt, the authorities indicate that a contract administrator should seek appropriate professional advice regarding design, workmanship or specification of materials if they touch on unfamiliar areas. It may be necessary to advise the client to seek their own professional advice or to limit the contractor's liability in the appropriate contract.

- When recommending contractors to a client, or accepting tenders on the client's behalf, a contract administrator should make investigations as to the competence and financial viability of the firm and its tender price.

PART 3:
Duties Typically Owed by Contract Administrators

9
Contractual and tortious duties

As set out in Part 2, a contract administrator's duties are most often defined by the terms of the contract under which he is engaged and these can be as different or as wide ranging as the nature of building contracts and the imaginations of the drafters of such contracts allow. However, some duties are more frequently undertaken by contract administrators than others.

Depending on the nature of the relationship between the contract administrator and his employer, duties that are concurrent with the contract may arise, for instance by virtue of a statute (i.e. an Act of Parliament or regulations made under an Act of Parliament) or a duty of care in tort (also often referred to as negligence). Further, those duties may be owed independently of the contract either to the employer or to third parties with whom the contract administrator has *no* contractual relationship at all. This might be by virtue of duties imposed by the common law (e.g. tort) or by an Act, such as the *Contracts (Rights of Third Parties) Act* 1999.

9.1 COMMON DUTIES OF CONTRACT ADMINISTRATORS

As set out above at 1.1, the list drawn up by the editor of *Hudson's Building Contracts* is a fairly comprehensive guide to the typical duties to be expected of a contract administrator. The following cases give a further flavour of contract administration work.

Jameson v Simon (1899)

A householder sued her architect for damages arising from dry rot to her property caused by the architect's failure properly to supervise its construction. The Scottish Court of Session held that an architect employed on the usual terms to plan and supervise the building of a house does not fulfil his duty of supervision merely by making occasional visits to the building and getting any parts of the work set right which he happens to observe on such visits are in disconformity to the contract; his duty is to give such supervision as will reasonably enable him to certify that the work of the contractors has been executed according to the contract.

An architect is not to be held responsible for all defective work that may be covered up in his absence. Not even a clerk of works could be expected to detect everything of that kind. When one contractor had to follow another and when the work done was about to be covered up so that it could not thereafter be inspected, the architect should, under the duty of supervision which he had undertaken, have ascertained either by personal inspection or through an assistant, whether the relevant work had been done according to specification.

Besides his design duties, the architect's work is just ordinary tradesman's work – drawing specifications and supervising the work. He is not supposed to do all the supervision personally. His subordinates can do much of it as well as he can himself, but if he undertakes to do it, he is bound either to do it himself or to have it done by some person whom he employs and in whom he has confidence. The meaning of the contract was that the architect was obliged to see that the work was done well before he certifies it. If he does not do this then the interest of the employer is altogether neglected.

Sandown Hotels Ltd v Phelps (1953)

An architect and surveyor were sued for negligent supervision of the painting of the exterior of a hotel. The architect argued that he had warned that the woodwork was saturated with salt so that the paint would not stay on, but he had been ordered to get the work done immediately. Neither the choice of paint, nor the specification was negligent. He said he had visited site daily and supervised adequately.

Held: There was no lack of care or skill in the drawing up of the specification. The choice of paint was not to blame. The architect was negligent in not giving sufficient attention to the preparation of the woodwork before the paint was applied and in failing to supervise the work adequately. The architect's evidence that he had warned about the danger of applying paint to the woodwork was rejected.

Cotton v Wallis (1955)

This case is also considered in chapters 3 and 7 and 6.1. Contract for the construction of a house on the standard RIBA form specified that materials and workmanship was to be to the satisfaction of the surveyor. The contractor was required to carry out works in accordance with the directions and to the reasonable satisfaction of the architect. The architect sued for his fees. The employer counterclaimed for damages for failing to exercise skill in supervising the erection of the house in that the work had been scamped.

The court held (Denning LJ dissenting) that, although the architect had no dispensing power to pass bad work, the low price of the building was a material factor in determining whether the architect could properly pass work as having been done to his reasonable satisfaction in accordance with the contract.

The standard of work required by a building contract depends on the terms of the contract. If, as in the present case, the contract provides that the works are to be carried out to the reasonable satisfaction of the architect, the low price of the building is a factor which may be taken into account in determining whether work may be passed by the architect as reasonably satisfactory, at any rate in relation to matters which, as here are small or trifling. In an action for negligence, an architect's skill may perhaps be measured by considering whether other experienced members of the profession would have acted similarly so that, although in the present case it was not held against the architect that other might have applied a stricter standard, the question of tolerance in building, down to a low price, must always be a question of degree.

East Ham Corporation v Bernard Sunley & Sons Ltd (1966)

Clause 24 of the RIBA contract (1950 edition) provided that an architect's final certificate after the expiry of the defects liability period was conclusive evidence of the sufficiency of the works and materials, save as regards all defects and insufficiencies in the works and materials which a reasonable examination would not have disclosed. The defendant contractors relied on clause 24 and argued that the whole of the their work under the contract was done under the supervision of the architect, the consulting engineer or the clerk of works and to their reasonable satisfaction. All the defects or faults now alleged were such that a reasonable examination should have disclosed them and accordingly, the architect's final certificate, was conclusive.

The House of Lords held that it is the architect's duty to issue the final certificate when the stipulated time arrives. The certificate is a certificate of value but, unless one of the exceptions apply, it is also to be conclusive evidence as to the sufficiency of the works and materials and, in view of clause 24(g), that is to be interpreted as meaning that they are in accordance with the contract.

Clause 24 meant the final certificate was indeed conclusive save in the exceptional circumstances stated and that even the express power of an arbitrator to open up and review or revise any certificate did not extend to opening up, reviewing or revising the final certificate.

The period during which such defects or faults should have been identified by the 'reasonable examination' in clause 24 was not limited to the date of practical completion or the end of the defects liability period but extended throughout the period of the contract works.

It was the duty of the architect generally to supervise the execution of the contract and to see that the work was properly done. To this end he could require the opening up for inspection of any work covered up. He and his representatives had the right to visit the works at all reasonable times and the contractor was under the duty to carry out such instructions as he might give.

Each month he had to certify the value of the work properly executed. It follows that at least once a month he had to examine the work done and satisfy himself that it had been properly done. Presumably he would keep himself informed of the progress of the work and, while the contract did not require him or his representatives to be always upon the site, he would regard it as his duty to go there or to send his representative there to inspect the sufficiency of the work done, particularly when an important stage of the building was being completed. He would, for instance, presumably want to satisfy himself that the foundations were in order before they were covered up.

On the occasions on which he inspected work done, whether for the purpose of issuing interim certificates or at other times, it was his duty on a reasonable examination to satisfy himself that the work had been properly done.

Given that the architect is not permanently on site, but only makes periodic visits, it is quite possible that, for whatever reason, the architect may fail to make an examination at an early stage of the building operation which would have disclosed some defect. Such a failure is not necessarily negligent – it may be due to no more than an error of judgment or a deliberately calculated risk that it was reasonable and proper to take.

If a clerk of works is employed by the building owner, he is under a duty to communicate matters which come to his attention to the architect. But he is not there as the representative of the architect: he has no architectural skills. The reasonable examination is one to be carried out by the architect, not the clerk of works.

William Tomkinson & Sons Ltd v The Parochial Church Council of St Michael and Others (1990)

The contract was in the form of the JCT agreement for minor works (1980 edition). The reported proceedings concerned the trial of preliminary issues, including:

- Were the contractors (the claimant) given notice of certain defects as required by clause 2.5 of the JCT conditions? Held: The contractor was given sufficient notice for the purposes of the clause. It was accepted that it was the architect's duty to pass on the employer's complaints about defects to the contractor and to investigate them for himself.

- Does clause 2.5 of the JCT conditions afford the contractor a defence to the church's claim for the cost of remedying certain defects having regard to the circumstances that those defects were remedied by other contractors on the instructions of the church prior to the date of practical completion? Held: The church was entitled to recover damages for defects that appeared before practical completion, but that the measure of damages was the cost which the contractor would have incurred in remedying the defects.

The court also addressed the requirement to confirm notification of defects in writing contained in clause 3.5 of the JCT contract. The question of whether a communication to the contractor constitutes sufficient notice depends on the wording of the relevant contractual clause. Clauses 2.5 and 3.5 of the JCT minor works do not specify any particular form for such a notice or say by whom it is to be given. Contrast clause 17 of the JCT form of main contract (1980 edition), which requires that notification of a defect be given *by the architect* and that it shall be delivered to the contractor in the form of a *schedule of defects* no later than 14 days after the expiry of the defects liability period.

Department of National Heritage v Steensen Varming Mulcahy (a firm) (1998)

A claim for professional negligence against mechanical and electrical engineers arising out of work on the British Library in London. Laing Management Ltd ('LM'), the management contractors for the project, were joined as third parties.

The defendant engineers claimed that the defects were caused by bad workmanship by others and/or bad supervision and lack of coordination by LM. The judge held that the plaintiffs failed to establish that the damage to the cabling was caused by negligence on the defendant's part. LM had responsibility for the inspection of the electrical and mechanical work during construction and installation.

The judge also considered the extent of SVM's liability for supervision and workmanship by the other contractors. Held: SVM's duty was to make such site visits as were reasonably likely to be required to ensure that the site was adequately supervised so that the electrical works would be properly executed in accordance with good engineering practice.

He held that SVM was under an obligation to do what it reasonably could to see that LM discharged its obligations as regards M&E services: in practice, if advice and admonition was insufficient, all that SVM could do was voice any concerns to the supervising officer.

SVM's duty did *not* extend to preventing the contractor from doing bad work: that could only be done by such close supervision as would be expected from a foreman. SVM's duties were limited to taking steps which would discourage bad work and if possible discover it after it had been done.

Royal Brompton Hospital Trust v Hammond and others (2002)

The House of Lords rejected a claim brought by the employer hospital against its architect for negligent certification of an extension of time. The case was decided on the basis of their Lordships' restrictive interpretation of section 1(1) of the *Civil Liability (Contribution) Act* 1978 (see further below), but a subsequent trial held simply on the question of negligent certification decided that the architect was liable to the employer for wrongfully granting an extension of time to a contractor which was undeserved and which had the effects both of depriving the employer of his right to liquidated damages and of exposing him to paying the contractor for the extra loss and expense incurred during the overrun of the contract period.

Great Eastern Hotel Co Ltd v John Laing Co. Ltd (2005)

This case has been addressed in Parts 2 and 3, 5.2 and chapter 8 above, but is worth referring to in this context as it is the first reported case on breach of obligation under a Construction Management Agreement. The defendant, John Laing, was employed under a management contract to oversee the procurement process in respect of refurbishment works to the Great Eastern Hotel in London. John Laing's responsibilities under the management contract encompassed the selection, administration and coordination of the works with a multitude of trade contractors. One of the terms of the management contract (specifically, clause 3.4) provided that John Laing was to 'procure that each Trade Contractor complies with all of its obligations under and all the requirements of their respective Trade Contracts'.

John Laing's failure to ensure that the individual trade packages were workable and complete meant that it was liable to reimburse the employer for the extra cost of having to order the omitted work as variations.

9.2 DUTY TO ACT FAIRLY

Although each contract must be construed on its own facts, where there is a provision in a building contract for a third party contract administrator to conduct the certification process, he will be required to act impartially and independently of both parties.

London Borough of Merton v Leach (1985)

In reviewing what terms could be implied into a construction contract, Vinelott J reviewed the position and responsibilities of the architect under the JCT form of contract (1963 edition). His review is applicable to all contract administrators as follows:

'It is to my mind clear that under the standard conditions the architect acts as the servant or agent of the building owner in supplying the contractor with the necessary drawings, instructions, levels and the like and in supervising the progress of the work and in ensuring that it is properly carried out. He will of course normally though not invariably have been responsible for the design of the work. There are very few occasions when a building owner himself is required to act directly without the intervention of the architect ... To the extent that the architect performs these duties, the building owner contracts with the contractor that the architect will perform them with reasonable diligence and with reasonable skill and care. The contract also confers on the architect discretionary powers which he must exercise with due regard to the interests of the contractor and the building owner. The building owner does not undertake that the architect will exercise his discretionary powers reasonably; he undertakes that although the architect may be engaged or employed by him he will leave him free to exercise his discretions fairly and without improper interference by him.

A contractor must be prepared to be willing to accept a contract which confers these discretionary powers on the servant or agent of the building owner firstly because the "architect/supervising officer" is normally a qualified architect (and if he is not he will be a responsible employee with experience of building works) and in either case will be under a duty to act fairly between the parties; secondly because ... his decision is subject to review by an arbitrator ...

As I have said, to the extent that the architect exercises these discretions his duty is to act fairly; "the building owner and the contractor make their contract on the understanding that in all such matters the architect will act in a fair and unbiased manner and it must therefore be implicit in the owner's contract with the architect that he shall not only exercise due care and skill but also reach such decisions fairly, holding the balance between his client and the contractor" (see *Sutcliffe v Thackrah* [1974] AC 727 per Lord Reid at p.737).'

Lubenham Fidelities v South Pembrokeshire DC (1986)

The council entered into a JCT Standard Form of Building Contract 1963 Edition contract for building works to a property. The original contractor went into liquidation and therefore the plaintiff finance company elected to perform the contract. The plaintiff instructed subcontractors to carry out the works but remained responsible to the defendant council for those works. The architects issued interim certificates that wrongly deducted monies in respect of liquidated damages and defective work. The council paid the plaintiff in accordance with the interim certificate. As a result, the plaintiff withdrew the new subcontractors from the site and the work ceased. Consequently, the council suffered losses.

The Court of Appeal considered the position of the parties in relation to the interim certificate. It held that:

1   the council were not in breach of contract by failing to pay in excess of the sum on the interim certificate. If the council paid the amount due in the certificate they fulfilled their obligation;

2   pursuant to the contract, it was a condition precedent to the contractor's entitlement to payment that the architect issued a certificate; and

3   the architects were not liable to the claimants for the shortfall between the sums due them and the sums actually paid to them in accordance with the certificate.

However, the court also cited with approval argument by the council's counsel which demonstrated the importance of the architects' role in making the arrangements between the employer and the building contractor really work. Although the architect is appointed by the employer, he does have a number of obligations throughout the contract when he has to act in a wholly disinterested and unbiased way in the interests of both parties.

For instance, under the JCT contract in question, works were to be completed to the reasonable satisfaction of the architect who was entitled to give far-reaching instructions to the contractor which might materially alter the nature and extent of the works. The architect had power to prevent unfixed materials delivered to the site from being removed from it. It is the architect who issued the certificate of practical completion and any extension of time that he considered to be due to the contractor. Besides making decisions on the subletting of works or the nomination of subcontractors, the architect also had the pre-eminent role in the certification of what payment had fallen due on an interim and final basis.

Such evidence of the architect's considerable authority to run the contract was accepted as supporting the existence of a duty to act fairly. Thus, where the architect issues a certificate the parties should be able to treat what it says on its face as binding unless and until an arbitrator held it to be bad, even where there was a patent error on the face of the certificate.

Costain Ltd v Bechtel Ltd (2005)

Costain and its consortium partners were concerned that Bechtel, the project manager, was encouraging its employees and consortium partners to issue certificates of sums due in a partial and unfair manner. It brought proceedings to prevent this and made an application for an interim injunction whilst those proceedings were pending. The question was: whether a project manager under an NEC form of contract was under a duty to act impartially when certifying works. The judge held that it was at least sufficiently arguable that such a duty exists and therefore granted the interim injunction sought.

Scheldebouw BV v St James Homes (Grosvenor Dock) Ltd (2006)

This case concerned the question whether the employer could replace the original construction manager and instate itself in the role after the commencement of the works or whether a duty to act impartially should prevent this.

The court set out four general propositions concerning the position and duties of the contract administrator (referred to as 'the decision maker'):

1   The precise role and duties of the decision maker will be determined by the terms of the contract under which he is required to act.

2   Generally the decision maker is not and cannot be regarded as independent of the employer.

3   When performing his decision making functions, the decision maker is required to act in a manner which has variously been described as independent, impartial, fair and honest. These concepts are overlapping but not synonymous. They connote that the decision maker must use his professional skills and his best endeavours to reach the right decision as opposed to a decision which favours the interests of the employer.

4   The fact that the decision maker acts in conjunction with other professionals when performing his decision making function does not water down his legal duty.

9.2.1 Summary

- Whilst each contract must be construed on its own facts, where there is provision for a contract administrator to conduct the certification process under a contract, he will be required to act impartially and independently of both parties to the contract in carrying out his certification duties (but possibly not other aspects of his work).

9.3 CONTRACTUAL DUTIES AND THIRD PARTIES

Non-parties to a contract usually cannot either rely on the rights created by the contract or be bound by the contractual obligations. As mentioned below, there is now a limited statutory exception to this rule created by the *Contracts (Rights of Third Parties) Act* 1999.

9.4 EFFECT OF SUPERVISION ON CONTRACTOR'S LIABILITY

Gallagher v McDowell Ltd (1961)

The defendant contractors constructed a residential property for the Northern Ireland Housing Trust and on completion it was inspected and passed by the Trust's architect. The plaintiff's husband was the first tenant of the house and he and his wife both moved in shortly after the inspection. Subsequently, the plaintiff suffered injury because a hole in a floor board had been inadequately patched up by the defendant. The plaintiff sued the defendant for damages for negligence.

On appeal, the Court of Appeal held that the defendant owed a duty to the plaintiff to take reasonable care in repairing the hole to avoid causing her physical injury.

The fact that the property had been subject to intermediate inspection by the developer's architect did not justify a reasonable expectation on the contractor's part that such inspection would expose the danger that inflicted damage on the plaintiff. The contractor was therefore still held to be liable to the plaintiff for breach of his duty of care, notwithstanding the architect's inspection process.

William Hill Organisation Ltd v Bernard Sunley & Sons Ltd (1982)

Where a contract so provides, a final certificate can be conclusive evidence that works are free from defects. This is the case even where there is a contractual obligation on the contractor to supervise its own work and therefore detect defects that the contractor's supervisor should reasonably have spotted. Such a contractual clause circumscribes the boundaries of the contractor's duties in tort.

The relevant clause in the contract provided that the architect's final certificate was to be 'conclusive evidence in any proceedings arising out of the contract that the works have been properly carried out and completed in accordance with the terms of the Contract', save for (a) fraud or (b) latent defects. Serious defects in the cladding appeared in the works between eight and 11 years after the issue of the final certificate by the plaintiff employer's architect. The employer claimed that the defects had been fraudulently concealed by the contractor so that the employer was bound neither by the expiry of the normal six-year limitation period nor the effect of the final certificate. The claim was dismissed because the employer failed to discharge the burden of proving fraudulent concealment. In so holding, the trial judge said that the employer had to show that their own supervising architect, in exercising reasonable skill and care, could not have been expected to have observed the defects.

The Court of Appeal upheld the decision: the employer was wrong to argue that the contractual obligation on the contractor to supervise its own work meant that the employer was entitled to rely on that obligation to found a case of fraudulent concealment. The question to be asked in relation to fraudulent concealment was: in all the circumstances, were the facts such that the conscience of the contractor of the subcontractor should have been so affected that it was unconscionable to proceed with the work or to cover up the defect without correcting it? It was not enough simply to show that the contractor had continued with the works (or been allowed to do so by the contract administrator) in such a way as to cover up a defect.

In any case, it was very unlikely that the architect, engineer or clerk of works could have observed that the works were not in accordance with the drawings and it was unreasonable to have expected them to have done so. This may have been inefficient on the part of such professionals but it was not sufficient to establish a case of fraudulent concealment.

EH Cardy v Taylor (1994)

The third party (unqualified) architects were engaged by the claimant contractor under a design and build contract for the development of a luxury hotel for the defendant developer. Payment of the fees of both the contractor and the architect was expressly contingent on the grant of planning permission. In the event, although some work was carried out, no planning permission was obtained that would have been suitable for the construction of a luxury hotel.

On the trial of the defendant's counterclaim for negligence against the contractor and the third party architect, it was held that it was negligent to design the building and submit the design without accurate site information. Accordingly, the developer was entitled to recover from the architects the diminution in the market value of the property caused by their negligence.

The liability of an unqualified architect was the same as would have been the responsibility of a qualified architect in similar circumstances. Since both the contractor and its architect undertook the same responsibilities and received the same instructions from the developer, any liability of the contractor was passed to or at least shared by the architect.

It was the duty of the contractor (and the architects on their behalf) to ascertain a detailed brief from the developer. To design a hotel extension they needed to know what sort and standard of hotel was required. Failing to find out that information was negligent.

The architects alleged that the contractor had been contributory negligent in failing to check that they had performed their work properly. The judge rejected this: There is little point hiring a professional to do work if it is to be said that the client has a duty to check the professional's work.

9.4.1 Summary

- The contractor cannot escape liability for defective work by blaming the contract administrator's failure to spot it and point it out.

- Similarly, the contract administrator cannot avoid or diminish his liability by blaming his employer for failing to check that the contact administrator had carried out his job properly.

9.5 EXCESS OF AUTHORITY

The contract administrator is capable of binding the employer to agreements, instructions and undertakings that he gives on the employer's behalf, so long as such agreements, instructions and undertakings are within the ostensible authority given to him by the employer. Where the contract administrator goes beyond that authority, the employer will not be bound and the contract administrator may be liable himself.

R v Peto (1826)

This case is also considered at 4.1 above. In the absence of an express power given to a surveyor to vary the works it was no answer to a claim of defective work that the contractor had followed the surveyor's instructions. There was no implied power for a surveyor to vary the works.

Pole v Leask (1862)

The extent and nature of the authority of an agent may be defined by writing, by oral instruction or by a course of dealing between the parties. When the authority to an agent is general, it will be construed liberally, but according to the usual course of business in the relevant industry.

Where an express authority is given, an authority is implied combined with it to do all acts which may be necessary for the purpose of effecting the object for which the express authority was given.

The agent's authority may be enlarged. This could happen where the principal knows of and allows the agent to carry out work on his behalf beyond the limits of the express authority originally granted. In such circumstances, the principal/employer will be held liable for his agent's acts and omissions committed on his behalf in accordance with the wider scope of authority to which he has acquiesced.

Ismail v Polish Ocean Lines (1976)

If an agent exceeds the authority of his employment, the employer is not liable for his acts unless there is apparent or ostensible authority. If there is apparent or ostensible authority, the employer will be prevented from denying the authority of his agent.

In this case, the agent concerned was acting on behalf of a charterer of a ship carrying potatoes from Egypt to England. Since the charterer had authorised his agent to give instruction as to how to stow the potatoes and since the agent had given express instructions as to their stowage, the charterer was estopped by his conduct from asserting that the stowage was defective.

Credit Lyonnais Bank Nederland v Export Credits (2000)

An employer is only liable for the wrongful acts of his employee, if those wrongful acts are committed during the course of the employee's employment. An employer should not be liable for acts of the servant or agent which are not performed within the course of the servant's employment or the agent's authority.

Thus, in this case, a government agency was held not to be liable to the claimant bank for a fraudulent transaction perpetrated by its employee, because such fraud was outside the course of the latter's employment.

Applying this principle to a construction context, the employer would not be liable to a third party for the default of his contractor or contract administrator if that default was not committed in the course of the contractor's employment or within the bounds of the contract administrator's authority as the employer's agent.

Kelner v Baxter (1866)

Where a party to a contract professes to be signing as an agent but in fact is *not* acting for a principal at the time of signing, he is personally liable on the contract. Whilst this case concerned a dispute over the sale of goods, the principle could apply to a construction project where, for instance, a contract administrator who has not yet been appointed by the employer purports to enter into agreements on his behalf. In such a case, the contract administrator risks assuming personal liability to the parties with which he contracts.

However, the employer can *subsequently* ratify such an unauthorised contract provided it was professedly made on the employer's behalf and provided the employer existed at the time the contract was made.

9.5.1 Personal liability

In normal circumstances, an employee or a director of a company will not be held personally liable for a breach of a contractual or tortious duty that he may commit during the course of his employment by his company. Accordingly, a contract administrator will not be personally liable to an employer if, on a proper interpretation of the contract of employment, the contracting party was the contract administrator's limited company rather than the individual himself. The same is true where by reason of a contractor's default, a contract administrator has been left exposed to paying damages to the employer: save in extreme cases (such as where the contract was induced by a fraudulent misrepresentation) or where on a proper construction the contract *was* made personally, the contract administrator may not seek redress against the contractor in a personal capacity, even if the contractor's company has gone into liquidation.

Convent Hospital Ltd v (1) Eberlin & Partners (2) Barrie Roberts Ltd (in liquidation) and (3) BW Roberts (1989)

The plaintiff employer entered into a contract with the second defendant (Barrie Roberts Ltd) for the construction of an extension to a hospital in Nottingham. However, nine months into the contract, the contractor became insolvent and appointed a receiver. The architects (Eberlin) had failed to ensure that the contractors had provided a performance bond before the contract was signed or thereafter, and the plaintiffs brought a successful action in negligence against Eberlin in negligence for that failure. Eberlin in turn attempted to recover its losses from the third defendant (Mr Roberts) who was the managing director of the contractor. Eberlin alleged that Mr Roberts had made or was party to making four misrepresentations either fraudulently or negligently which he knew to be false in order to induce Eberlin to allow or advise the plaintiffs to enter into the construction contract.

The claim was rejected in the Official Referees' Court and also on appeal. The court held that the claim was not made out because:

- the first representation relied on was not made fraudulently, but was simply a statement of the price for which a bond could be purchased;
- Mr Roberts himself was not a party to the second representation, which, although fraudulent, was made by his quantity surveyor;
- the third and fourth fraudulent misrepresentations were made by Mr Roberts and were fraudulent but they did not induce the plaintiffs to enter into the construction contract.

9.5.2 Summary

- The contract administrator may bind his employer to agreements, instructions and undertakings that he gives on the employer's behalf, so long as such agreements, instructions and undertakings are within the ostensible authority given to him by the employer.
- Where the contract administrator goes beyond that authority, the employer will not be bound and the contract administrator may be liable himself.
- Where the contracting party is a company, a director or employee of that company will not usually be held personally liable for defaults committed by him as part of his employment.

9.6 DELEGATION

In certain circumstances (and depending on the terms of his engagement), the contract administrator may delegate certain of his functions to others: for instance, to a clerk of works or quantity surveyor. However, unless otherwise specifically agreed with the employer, the contract administrator will be liable for acts and omissions committed by such people as if they were the acts and omissions of the contract administrator himself.

Saunders & Collard v Broadstairs (1890)

A finding of 'extraordinary' and 'disgraceful' negligence was made against architects engaged (amongst other things) to supervise construction of a drainage scheme. The fact that the employer also engaged an incompetent clerk of works (on whom the architect relied, knowing he was incompetent) was no defence.

Lee v Lord Bateman (1893)

Where the architect accepted the (wrong) view of the clerk of works as to the sufficiency of certain beams without himself carrying out an inspection, he was negligent if the beams turned out to be insufficient. Reliance on the clerk of works was not a defence.

Florida Hotels v Mayo (1965)

On a typical works project where an architect was engaged to provide periodical supervision, the court held that he was not obliged personally to check every detail but he would be in breach of his obligations if he failed to inspect the most important parts of the construction (in this case the formation of a concrete support slab for a swimming pool).

Whilst evidence of normal architectural practice on such a job was judged to be useful by the court, it was not decisive of the legal obligations undertaken by an architect on a particular job. The architects were therefore held to be bound to supervise and inspect the works with due care and attention and in particular to oversee the pouring of concrete to form the slabs before it was covered up. The architects had not supervised this obligation where they relied on workmen to tell them when the concrete was to be poured since they were employed to supervise the same workmen they purported to rely upon. Periodic inspection did not mean that the architects were engaged only to supervise such work as could be seen on the particular days of their routine inspections or to attend to supervise only when advised that an occasion demanding their supervision had arisen. Rather, they were bound to make reasonable arrangements of a reliable nature to ensure they were kept informed of the general progress of the work and, in particular, to be notified of the readiness of the formwork and the placement of reinforcement for the pouring of the concrete. Such arrangements ought to have included clear and express instructions to the foreman that work of the kind in question should not be covered up until the respondents had inspected it or at least had an adequate opportunity to inspect it.

Leicester Board of Guardians v Trollope (1911)

The employer engaged both an architect (the defendant) and a clerk of works. The clerk of works fraudulently allowed the builder to lay the floor defectively. The architect relied entirely on the clerk of works in this regard and so failed to observe the defect in construction. The architect was negligent and could not rely as a defence on the fact that the employer had engaged a fraudulent clerk of works.

It was observed that the distinction between the clerk of works and the architect was that the clerk of works is expected to deal with matters of detail while the architect is not. However, on the facts the architect had failed to see that an important part of his design was carried out properly.

Kensington & Chelsea & Westminster v Wettern Composites (1984)

The claimant engaged (as independent contractors) the defendant architects and engineers on the project to extend a hospital. It also employed (as its servant) a clerk of works.

Although the clerk of works had been negligent in overlooking certain defects, this did not reduce the architect's liability to use reasonable skill and care to ensure conformity with design as opposed to matters of detail.

However, because the employer was vicariously liable for the contributory negligence of the clerk of works, damages against the architect were reduced by 20 per cent to account for this.

Moresk Cleaners Ltd v Hicks (1966)

The plaintiffs employed the defendant architects to design an extension to its laundry business. The design of the building was found to be defective. However, the architects had purported to delegate the design to a third party and argued that it should not be liable because it was an implied term of its employment that it could delegate specialised design tasks to qualified subcontractors or alternatively that it had implied authority to act as the plaintiffs' agent to employ the third party.

These arguments were rejected. The architect had no power to delegate its design duties and no implied authority to employ the third party to design the building. A building owner who entrusts the task of designing a building to an architect is entitled to look to that architect to see that the building is properly designed. The architect has no power whatever to delegate his duty to anybody else.

As to the alternative argument, it was essential that, if the architects wished to employ a third party to do its work, it should obtain the permission of the building owner before doing so. In the absence of such permission, there was no implied authority to engage a third party as the plaintiffs' agent.

Consideration was given to the question of what an architect or other consultant should do where he was asked to carry out specialist or cutting-edge work which was beyond his capabilities. It was held that if the consultant was not able to do the work himself he had three courses open to him:

1   he could inform the employer that he was unqualified and reject the job;

2   he could inform the employer that he was unqualified and request the employer to employ a suitable specialist to carry out the aspect of the work he could not do himself;

3   he could employ a specialist himself. Whilst doing so would not absolve the consultant of liability to the employer for the work, he would have the reassurance of knowing that if he acts upon the advice given by the specialist and it turns out to be wrong, the specialist will owe the same duty to him as he, the consultant, owes to the employer.

London Borough of Merton v Lowe (1981)

The claimant engaged the defendant architects under the RIBA conditions to design and supervise the erection of a new indoor swimming pool. The architects specified the use of a proprietary product (Pyrok) for the construction of the ceilings and subcontracted its design and construction to Pyrok Ltd.

Cracks were later found in the ceilings of nine rooms, but this did not prompt the architect to carry out further investigation into the standard of construction of the ceiling in the main pool room. The architect then issued the final certificate under the building contract which incorporated the JCT Standard Form of Building Contract (1963 edition). Subsequently, it became apparent that the ceiling in the main pool was seriously defective and unsafe.

The court held that the architects had breached their contractual and tortious duties towards the claimant in not undertaking a proper investigation from the beginning. Although cracks in one patch of ceiling might not have been sufficient to put a reasonable architect on notice of a more widespread problem, the extent of the defects found prior to the issue of the final certificate should have raised suspicion that the fault was not isolated but ran throughout the building. The architects were found to be under a continuing duty to check that their design would work in practice and to correct any errors which may emerge. If their design was faulty, the architects would not be discharging their duty simply by ensuring that the contractor implemented that design faithfully.

By issuing the final certificate the architects had caused loss to the employer, namely the loss of the right of action against the main contractor who could rely on the final certificate as a defence to a claim for defects. The fact that the employer might have commenced proceedings against another party (such as a claim in tort against the subcontractor roofing specialists) was not relevant.

However, the architects had been entitled to delegate the design of the ceiling. Unlike in *Moresk* , the architects had not delegated their entire design obligation to a subcontractor but only a specialised aspect of the design. The decision to use Pyrok was reasonable in the circumstances.

McDermid v Nash Dredging Ltd (1987)

In this shipping case, the House of Lords held that an employer was not entitled to delegate its duty to take reasonable care to devise a safe system of work and to see that it was operated, notwithstanding that the system that they had devised was being implemented by a third party tug-boat owner.

In the same way, it is thought that an employer or main contractor would not escape liability for his duty of care to his contractor or subcontractor simply because he had appointed a contract administrator or architect to oversee the implementation of a safe working system. That does not mean that the contract administrator would necessarily escape liability. He may be liable to the employer by way of contribution (see 10.7 below).

Richard Roberts v Douglas Smith Stimson (1988)

The claimant employed the defendant architects to design alterations to its dyeworks at Hinckley. The architects had acted previously for the claimant on a similar project where a specialist consultant engineer had been retained to design the effluent tank. On this project, no such engineer was retained, but it was understood that if the architects needed technical advice beyond their own experience, they could obtain it from the claimant's own in-house expertise. The architects obtained a quotation from a specialist supplier for the tank lining, which both the claimant and the architects approved.

Following construction, the lining of the effluent tank failed. The claimant sued the architects for damages for breach of contract and negligence in recommending or permitting the choice of tank lining used and in issuing the final certificate despite the existence of the defect.

The court held that if the architects had wished to limit their role and/or liability, they should have done so expressly and in writing. They were responsible for the choice of tank lining and had failed properly to investigate its adequacy.

Part of their expertise as architects was to be able to collect information about materials of which they lacked knowledge and/or experience and to form a view about them. However, if they found themselves unable to form a reliable judgment about the tank lining, they should have informed the claimant and advised it to seek alternative specialist advice.

There was no finding of contributory negligence, despite the fact that the claimant had also approved the choice of tank lining. The architects had been employed to provide advice on the design and the claimant was entitled to rely on them. There was no point employing them otherwise.

Eames v North Herfordshire DC (1980)

Differential settlement affected a warehouse building in Hitchin, Herts. The judge found that a proper investigation at the time of the building's construction would have indicated that simple shallow foundations specified for use throughout the building would be bound to lead to serious, uneven and continuing settlement and substantial damage. On the facts the contractor, the architect, the original developers and the local authority were all in breach of their respective duties in the design and construction of the building.

As to the architect, the judge held that he could not shed his responsibility for the design of the foundations by ascertaining what will get by the local authority's requirements. In particular, where as here the architect was on notice that the local authority's recommendation for the design of the foundations might be inappropriate for the nature of the ground conditions, he was under an obligation to ascertain for himself whether the ground was suitable for the suggested foundations.

Moon v Witney Guardians (1837)

An architect had a right to employ a quantity surveyor and to pass the cost of employing him on to the employer, where the employer has authorised the architect to obtain tenders and where such tenders could only be obtained if quantities were prepared and issued. Whilst this accorded with usual industry practice in the early nineteenth century, it probably cannot be relied on as being applicable to current practice and norms. It is submitted that it will depend on the terms of the architect's engagement whether he will be required to cover the cost of employing a quantity surveyor himself or whether he is entitled to recover payment from the employer.

Clemence v Clarke (1880)

Where the contract between the employer and the contractor contains provision for measurement by a skilled quantity surveyor, an architect is not, in the absence of other factors, in breach of his duty to the employer if he relies on such measurements.

If the architect is entrusted with the general direction and superintendence of work, it is not reasonable that he should be expected to go over every aspect of other parties' work in detail. That would not only be impractical but in some cases (e.g. quantity surveying) would be outside the scope of most architects' expertise.

RB Burden v Swansea Corp (1957)

This is a further example of a case where the architect was held to have a right to rely on the work of a third party quantity surveyor appointed by the employer in carrying out his work as the certifier under a building contract.

The termination provisions of a building contract gave the contractor a right to determine the contract if the employer interfered with or obstructed the issue of an interim certificate by the architect. At the request of the architect, the employer instructed an independent quantity surveyor to make periodic valuations of the contractor's work. In reliance on one such valuation, the architect subsequently issued an interim certificate for payment of a significantly lesser sum than that for which the contractor had applied. The contractor determined the contract on the ground that the actions of the surveyor amounted to interference or obstruction by the employer with the issue of a certificate.

The House of Lords held that the employer had not interfered with or obstructed the issue of a certificate, since it had given no instructions that impeded the architect in performing his certification duties. Although the surveyor had not done his work properly, his negligence did not amount to interference.

Priestly v Stone (1888)

This case was primarily concerned with the question of whether a quantity surveyor appointed by the employer or his architect could be liable for errors in his estimates of quantities to the contractor either in contract or for misrepresentation. The Court of Appeal held that he could not be so liable: the quantity surveyor had no contract with the builder and had no control over whom his work was used by other than his employer. In preparing his quantities and passing them to the architect, the quantity surveyor was not making a representation to the contractor that they are true – only to the architect.

Further, whilst the architect would be entitled to rely on the quantity surveyor's work, if the quantities were *grossly* wrong, the architect would be negligent and liable to the employer if he failed to identify the errors.

Nye Saunders v Alan E Bristow (1987)

The claimant architects were engaged by the defendant to prepare and submit a planning application for proposed renovation of his substantial house. The defendant informed the architects that he had about £250,000 available to spend on the project. The defendant asked the architects to provide a written estimate of the likely costs of the works. The architects employed a quantity surveyor and sent to the claimant an estimate of £238,000 based on the latter's work. However, the quantity surveyor had failed to allow for increases caused by inflation or contingencies and the architects failed to point that out to the defendant.

Subsequently, when planning permission had been obtained and the initial design work progressed, it became apparent that the estimated cost of the project had escalated sharply to £440,000. The defendant cancelled the project, terminated the architects' employment and refused to pay their fees.

The architects' action to recover their fees was dismissed on the ground that they had failed in their duty to the defendant to take reasonable care in providing the projected estimate of costs. The Court of Appeal held:

- the cause of the increase in costs was inflation, about which the architects had failed to warn the defendant;

- since as at February 1974, it was not an accepted practice amongst a reasonable body of architects to avoid giving a warning as to inflation when providing an approximate estimate of a project's costs, the architects had been negligent;

- whilst it was acceptable and even prudent for the architects to consult a quantity surveyor to help provide the estimate, they could not avoid responsibility for their failure to draw the attention of the employer to the fact that the estimate did not take into account the likely effects of inflation;

- the duty to warn the employer of those effects rested on the architects and could not be avoided by passing it on to the quantity surveyor.

Try Build Ltd v Invicta Leisure Tennis Ltd (2000)

Contractors undertook to construct a tennis hall under a JCT 1981 design and build contract. Engineers who had been initially engaged by the employer were subsequently novated to the employment of the contractors. The swimming pool roof was of a novel design and, following construction, it failed. It was agreed that the primary cause of the failure was an insecure edging strip which was vulnerable to tears because the foil used was too thin.

Under the novation agreement, the engineers undertook an express duty to the contractor to exercise reasonable skill and care in the performance of its professional duties, including those carried out prior to the novation.

The court held that the engineers bore responsibility for the failure of the roof. It was an important part of the structure and the engineers were structural as well as civil design engineers. Given its cutting-edge design and the obvious importance of water-proofing, the engineers should have taken special care in their design and supervision of its construction.

Accordingly, the engineers were liable to indemnify the contractors.

Baxall Securities Ltd v Sheard Walshaw Partnership (2002)

On facts set out at 10.4.1 below, the cause of two floods in a warehouse was found to be a patent defect (the absence of overflows) which should have been spotted by the claimants' surveyors. The claimants' failure to identify the defect broke the chain of causation between the defendants' original negligent design and the damage suffered by the claimants.

9.6.1 Summary

- Depending on the terms of his engagement, the contract administrator may delegate certain of his functions to others.
- Unless otherwise specifically agreed with the employer, the contract administrator will be liable for acts and omissions committed by people to whom he has delegated or subcontract his work.

10
Duty of care

Besides the express and implied duties that a contract administrator owes to his employer under the terms of his contract, he will usually owe a concurrent duty to the employer to carry out his work with the reasonable skill and care to be expected of a competent contract administrator in all the circumstances of the particular project.

If his work is not done with reasonable skill and care, the contract administrator will be liable to compensate the employer for his negligence. This can be an important consideration in relation to the time-limits in which a legal claim can be brought.

In addition, a duty of care may be owed by the contract administrator to other interested parties, such as the contractor, a subcontractor or the owner/occupier of a building. The existence of such a duty of care depends on the proximity of the relationship between the parties, the foreseeability of damage, and whether in all the circumstances it is fair just and reasonable to impose it.

10.1 TESTS FOR EXISTENCE OF DUTIES OF CARE

Hedley Byrne v Heller (1964)

The appellant agents had placed advertising orders for a company on terms by which they, the appellants, were personally liable for the cost of the orders. In view of that risk, they asked their bankers to inquire into the company's financial stability and their bankers duly made inquiries of the respondents, who were the company's own bank. The respondents gave favourable references, but stipulated that they did so 'without responsibility'. In reliance on the references, the appellants placed orders that resulted in them incurring a substantial loss. They brought an action against the respondent bank for negligence in providing the references.

The House of Lords held that a negligent, though honest, misrepresentation (oral or in writing) may give rise to an action for damages for economic loss in tort, because the law will imply a duty of care. Where (a) a defendant assumes responsibility to a claimant by providing information or making a representation (which might be made as part of contract administration duties) to that claimant and (b) the claimant reasonably relies on that information or those services, it was fair, just and reasonable to impose liability in tort for the damage caused by negligent advice.

Murphy v Brentwood District Council (1991)

There is no general duty of care owed by contractors (unlike construction professionals) in tort in respect of defective construction work as it represents pure economic loss.

A contractor owes a duty to take reasonable care to avoid injury or damage, through defects in construction, to the persons or property of those whom he ought to have in mind as likely to suffer injury or damage. Such persons include subsequent owners or occupiers of a building constructed by builders, even though there was no contractual relationship between the builder and the owner/occupier. This liability is concurrent with the duties the contractor expressly and impliedly undertakes to the employer under the contract.

However, this liability only extends to latent defects and does not include damage that is purely economic loss. Where a defect was discovered before any injury to person or health or damage to property other than the defective house itself had occurred, the cost incurred by a subsequent purchaser of the property in putting right the defect was pure economic loss and therefore irrecoverable in tort. Liability is limited to damage to persons or property other than the subject of their work itself. For policy reasons, if the damage in respect of which the claim is brought relates to the subject of the contractor's work itself it is excluded as pure economic loss. Such damages can only be recovered for breach of or under a term of a contract.

A local authority (or an administrator acting for one), charged with supervising compliance with the building regulations or bye-laws, would not as a matter of public policy be held to owe a duty of care to a purchaser of a property to carry out those duties in such a way as to avoid causing the purchaser to suffer economic loss.

Henderson v Merrett Syndicates Ltd (1995)

Unlike contractors, professional consultants (such as engineers and architects) owe their contractual clients a concurrent and coextensive duty of care in tort in relation to the provision of their services.

To establish a duty of care in tort (and thereby a claim in negligence), a claimant must show:

- the existence of a duty of care in law;
- conduct which fell below the required standard by the defendant;
- a causative link between the defendant's conduct and the damage suffered by the claimant; and
- foreseeability that conduct of the type committed by the defendant was likely to cause damage of the type claimed.

Marc Rich v Bishop Rock Marine (1996)

The question whether a duty of care is owed by one party to another, depends on the questions of:

- the proximity of the parties' relationship;
- the foreseeability of the damage caused;
- whether it is fair just and reasonable to impose a liability on the defendant.

10.1.1 Summary

- In order to make a successful claim in tort, a claimant must show:

- the existence of a duty of care;
- conduct on behalf of the defendant that falls below the requisite standard;
- that the defendant's conduct caused the losses suffered;
- that it was reasonably foreseeable that the defendant's conduct would cause the losses suffered.

- The principal test for the existence of a duty of care is based on considerations of proximity between the parties, foreseeability of the damage caused and whether it is fair just and reasonable to impose such a duty.

- Generally, claims in tort will only succeed where the damage sustained is actual physical injury to person or property other than the property which is itself the product of the negligence.

- Whilst claims in tort for pure economic loss will not usually succeed, there are exceptions.

- A duty of care to avoid causing economic loss may arise where a party assumes responsibility to another by making a statement or providing information on which the other party reasonably relies.

10.2 DUTIES OF CARE IN THE CONSTRUCTION FIELD

Steljes v Ingram (1903)

An action against an architect for negligent supervision was an action founded in *contract* rather than tort. It is doubtful that the general common law attaches standard duties to an architect's profession, but even if it does the duty of supervision would not fall within the general scope of that duty.

Sharpe v ET Sweeting & Son Ltd (1963)

A contractor built a number of residential properties for a developer. The contractor was held liable to a tenant of the developer when, on completion, a reinforced concrete canopy collapsed on top of the tenant's wife. The contractor owed a duty of care to the tenant and other occupiers of the properties to take reasonable care to avoid causing injuries through defective work.

Voli v Inglewood Shire Council (1963) (High Court of Australia)

The defendant architect was employed by the council to design and supervise the construction of a local community hall. It was an express term of the contract that the defendant architect's plans had to be submitted to the Public Works Department and the Department of Health ('the Departments') for approval, before the works began. The architect defendant completed the plans and submitted them to the Departments. The plans were approved. It later transpired that the design of the hall was defective because the central joists that had been used were not of a sufficient size for their intended purpose. As a result of the defect, the hall stage collapsed and a number of people were injured. Those injured commenced proceedings against a number of parties, including the defendant architect.

The High Court of Australia considered the architect's duties under the contract, and in particular whether an architect is liable in negligence to a person who suffers harm by reason of faults in the design and construction.

The court held that in performing his duties under the contract, the architect was bound to act with due care, skill and diligence. The standard of this skill was held to be the standard of skill that is 'usual' among architects. The fact that the contract provided for the plans to be submitted to the Departments for approval before the works commenced, did not free the architect from liability. The submission of the plans to the Departments did not mean that they would correct the architect's mistakes.

The court also held that an architect is liable to anyone that could reasonably have been foreseen to be injured as a result of the architect's negligence. In this respect physical injury is treated differently from economic damage for which, as discussed further below, the range of people who can recover their losses in tort is limited.

Esso Petroleum Co. Ltd v Mardon (1976)

A counterclaim for negligent misrepresentation and/or breach of warranty by a tenant of a petrol station succeeded against the lessor oil company because the oil company's representation made by its representative during pre-contractual negotiations of the potential throughput of the petrol station was made negligently and/or in breach of the warranty.

The statement was a negligent representation made by a party who held itself out as having special expertise in circumstances that gave rise to a duty to take reasonable care to see that the representation was correct.

The statement also amounted to a warranty as to the potential throughput of the petrol station, in that it was a crucial matter made by a party who had or professed to have special knowledge and skill and was made with the intention of inducing the tenant to enter into the contract.

The measure of damages was the same whether the action was founded in contract or in tort, i.e. the damages that the defendant had lost by being induced to enter into the contract.

Oldschool and another v Gleeson (Construction) Ltd and others (1977)

The plaintiff owners entered into a contract with the first defendants, building contractors, and second defendants, consulting engineers, for the redevelopment of two houses. The works required the total demolition of one of the properties and the partial demolition of the other. During the demolition works the party wall separating one of the plaintiff owners' properties with their neighbour's properties collapsed, thereby resulting in damage to the neighbouring property. The plaintiff owners sued the first defendant and second defendants for indemnity against the damages that may be awarded in respect of the damage to the neighbouring property. The first defendants admitted liability and sought to recover a contribution from the second defendants on the basis that the second defendants owed them a duty of care for the design and/or supervision of the works and that by failing to provide an adequate design and/or supervision, the second defendants had breached that duty of care.

HHJ William Stabb QC considered whether a consulting engineer owes a duty of care to a building contractor, and if so, to what the scope of that duty is. He held that:

1   a consulting engineer does not have a duty to instruct the building contractor on how to do their work. The consulting engineer can offer advice to the building contractor; however, it is the responsibility of the building contractor to achieve the consulting engineer's design;

2   where a consulting engineer knows or ought to know that there is a risk of damage to a property, by reason of the building contactor's execution of the design, then the consultant engineer has a duty to warn the building contractor to take the necessary precautions.

Therefore, a consulting engineer will breach his duty to the building contractor if he fails to warn the building contractor to take the necessary precautions to abate the risk of damage occurring to a property.

Simaan General Contracting Co. v Pilkington Glass Ltd (No. 2) (1988)

The plaintiffs were the main contractors for a building in Abu Dhabi. The main contract specified the incorporation of curtain walling double-glazed units of green glass which were manufactured by the defendants. The plaintiffs subcontracted the erection of the curtain walling to a third party company. When the units had been installed, the architect rejected the units as being defective by reason of discrepancies in colouring. The plaintiffs brought an action in negligence against the defendants, alleging that by reason of the defects in the glass units they had suffered economic loss in that payment they would otherwise have received from the employer had been withheld.

The Court of Appeal found that the defendants did not owe the plaintiff a duty of care to avoid defects in the units which had caused them economic loss. Such a claim could only have succeeded if the plaintiff could show a special relationship between himself and the defendant which amounted to reliance by the plaintiff on the defendant (of the kind recognised *Hedley Byrne v Heller* (1964) considered above). The plaintiffs had required the third party curtain wall erectors to buy the glass from the defendants but only because they had a contractual obligation to do so. The defendants had not assumed a direct responsibility to the plaintiffs for the quality of the glass, accordingly there was no reason to depart from the normal contractual chain of liability.

Eckersley and others v Binnie and others (1988)

The first defendants were consultant engineers that designed an aqueduct for the third defendants, North West Water Authority ('the Authority'). The second defendants were tunnelling contractors that constructed the aqueduct between 1972 and 1975, under the supervision of the first defendants. Post 1975 the Authority were responsible for operating the aqueduct. In May 1984 an explosion occurred in the valve house, killing 16 visitors and injuring many others. Proceedings were commenced on behalf of those injured or killed in the explosion against the three defendants for negligence.

The Court of Appeal considered the duties of care owed by each of the defendants for the design, construction and operation of the tunnel. It held that:

1   At the design stage, the consultant engineer is expected to exercise the skill of a reasonably competent engineer specialising in the particular field of construction. In the circumstances, a reasonably competent engineer specialising in the design of water systems ought to have detected a risk of methane being present in the aqueduct. The explosion was therefore reasonably foreseeable. The first defendants were negligent in failing to take into account the possibility that methane may be present when designing the aqueduct;

2   The second defendants, the tunnelling contractors, did not owe the claimants a duty of care. The duty of care owed by the second defendants was to ensure that the

aqueduct was safe for those that used it during its construction. It did not continue upon the completion of construction.

3   The third defendants were not negligent towards the plaintiffs. The Authority was unaware that the first defendants had been negligent at the design stage. Therefore, the explosion was not foreseeable to the Authority.

Day v Ost (New Zealand) (1973)

The New Zealand Supreme Court considered an allegation that an architect had assumed a duty of care to a subcontractor by giving him an assurance that he would be paid by the employer.

The plaintiff, a block-laying and plastering subcontractor, stopped work because he had not been paid. The defendant architect requested the plaintiff to resume work and assured him that he would receive the progress payment of $1,000 and that the employer had ample funds to cover the balance of his contract price. In reliance on this assurance, the plaintiff completed the work but received only the progress payment, not the rest of his contract price.

The court held that by, giving this assurance, the defendant had voluntarily assumed a responsibility towards the plaintiff to take reasonable care that his assurance was true. In fact, the defendant had been aware that the employer had *not* set aside sufficient money to cover the plaintiff's contract price. Accordingly, the defendant was liable for breach of a duty of care to the plaintiff. The measure of damages was the loss suffered by the plaintiff after resuming work.

Pacific Associates Inc v Baxter (1990)

The plaintiffs were contractors carrying out dredging and reclamation work to a lagoon in the Persian Gulf. The plaintiffs' contract with the employer provided for the defendants, who were engineers, to carry out pre-contract reports on the ground conditions, to supervise the plaintiffs' work and to administer the payment provisions of the contract.

The plaintiffs issued a writ against the defendants for damages for economic loss, claiming that, by their failure to certify sums sought by the plaintiffs and by their rejection of the plaintiffs' claim against the employer, the defendants had been negligent or breached their obligation to act fairly and impartially in administering the contract.

The court held that that although the defendants were professional engineers, employed to supervise the plaintiffs' work, they were acting solely for the employer in doing so and were not under the terms of the contract or otherwise obliged to exercise due care to the plaintiffs. They had not voluntarily accepted any further duty to the plaintiffs and so did not owe a duty to avoid causing economic loss to the plaintiffs.

In the absence of a voluntary assumption of responsibility by the defendants to the plaintiffs, the contractual chain of liability (and especially the inclusion of a clause in the main contract disclaiming any liability owed by the defendants to the plaintiffs) was incompatible with the finding of a duty of care in tort.

This appears to overturn earlier authority which implied that such a duty might be owed (e.g. *Michael Saliss v Calil* (1987)).

Gloucestershire Health Authority v Torpy (1997)

The standard of care to be expected from specialist engineers may be more onerous than general practice engineers.

Samuel Payne v John Setchell Ltd (2002)

The court confronted the apparent anomaly that the duty of care owed to employers by contractors had been held to be more limited than that owed by professional consultants. The court attempted to narrow the scope of the duty owed by professional consultants (as found in *Henderson v Merrett* (1995), considered above) to make it coterminous with the duty owed by contractors. The court held that *both* a contractor and an engineer should ordinarily owe a tortious duty to take reasonable care against causing their contractual client personal injury or damage to property other than to the building or construction work that is itself the subject of their work or services (i.e. pure economic loss remains excluded).

Mirant Asia Pacific v Ove Arup (2005)

The court declined to follow *Samuel Payne v Setchell* (above) and applied the test set down by the House of Lords in *Henderson v Merret* (1995) on the scope of a professional consultant's duties. Thus, an engineer owed a concurrent duty of care to his client in contract *and* tort in respect of economic losses referable to design errors.

10.2.1 Summary

- A professional consultant, such as a contract administrator, owes a concurrent duty of care to his client in contract and tort to avoid causing him economic loss.
- A contractor does not owe such a concurrent duty of care in tort to his client.
- A party will be liable in damages where it holds itself out as having special expertise in circumstances and negligently makes a false statement which is foreseeably relied upon by another party.
- Usually the contractual chains of liability commonly employed in building projects are incompatible with a finding of a duty of care owed by parties who are not in direct contractual relationships with each other. However, there are exceptions and this is explored in more detailed below (see 10.4 and 10.6).

10.3 STANDARD OF CARE REQUIRED

A mistake by a professional man may or may not amount to negligence. If the majority of the profession would under the circumstances have done the same thing, this is usually a good defence.

Where you get a situation which involves the use of some special skill or competence (such as a contract administrator's duties), then the test as to whether there has been negligence or not is the standard of the ordinary skilled man exercising and professing to have that special skill. In other words, quantity surveyors, architects and engineers will be judged by the standards to be expected of a reasonable member of their respective professions faced with the circumstances that they find themselves in.

Where there is no one accepted practice followed by the majority of a particular profession, the professional will not be held to have been negligent if he can show that he acted in accordance with a practice accepted as proper by a *reasonable* body of professionals in his field, even if others of his colleagues disagree.

Jameson v Simon (1899)

The Scottish Court of Session considered the extent of an architect's duty to inspect on a project where there were multiple individual contractors.

If the nature of the contract imposes a duty on the contract administrator to exercise special care, for instance by inspecting the work of a contractor prior to it being covered up by another contractor's work, then it is not sufficient for the contract administrator to say that he has done what was customary or accepted as the applicable industry standard, if he fails to inspect in accordance with that express duty.

Bolam v Friern Hospital Management Committee (1957)

Although this case concerned medical negligence, it is widely accepted that it sets out the test by which professional negligence in all fields is judged. Giving judgment, McNair defined 'negligence' as follows:

'In an ordinary case it is generally said that you judge that [i.e. negligence] by the action of the man in the street. He is an ordinary man. In one case it has been said that you judge it by the conduct of the man on the top of a Clapham omnibus. He is an ordinary man. But where you get a situation which involves the use of some special skill or competence, then the test whether there has been negligence or not is not the test of the man on the top of a Clapham omnibus, because he has not go this special skill. The test is the standard of the ordinary skilled man exercising and professing to have that special skill. A man may not possess the highest expert skill at the risk of being found negligent. It is well established law that it is sufficient if he exercises the ordinary skill of an ordinary competent man exercising that particular art ... A doctor is not negligent if he is acting in accordance with a practice accepted as proper by a responsible body of medical men skilled in that particular art.'

A similar test applies to the standard of care expected of a contract administrator.

East Ham v Bernard Sunley (1966)

The architect is not expected to be on site permanently but only to appear at intervals. Given the variety of the architects' duties when he does attend site (e.g. dealing with delays and labour troubles, checking suppliers and unforeseen ground conditions), he is not expected to make a minute inspection of the builder's work to see that the builder is complying with the specification. Therefore, even if the architect fails to discover a defect that would have been disclosed by a reasonable examination of the work, the architect will not necessarily be held to have been negligent.

Further, their Lordships rejected the suggestion that the parties to a building contract (the 1950 RIBA form) contemplated that the builder should be excused liability for faulty work merely because the architect had failed to carry out an examination during the currency of the works which would have disclosed the defect.

Greaves & Co. v Baynham Meikle (1975)

An architect's (or other contract administrator's) liability is not in normal circumstances absolute. He does not face strict liability to the extent that he would be liable whenever loss results from his acts or omissions. It must be shown that he has been negligent or breached the terms of his engagement in a material way. Thus, the implication of a fitness for purpose obligation in an architect's retainer is highly unusual if all the architect is supplying is professional advice or designs.

Sutcliffe v Chippendale (1982)

In a case in which there was no formal contract between the architect and the employer and where the contractor had entered insolvency after taking the benefit of interim certificates despite there being numerous defects in his work, the court (HHJ Stabb QC) considered the extent to which the architect owed the employer a duty of care.

The judge found that an architect's duty to supervise the contractor's work required him to follow the progress of the work and to take steps to see that the works complied with the general requirements of the contract and the specification.

In exercising his duties of certification, the architect was required to notify the quantity surveyor in advance of any work which he classified as not properly executed so as to give the quantity surveyor an opportunity to exclude it from the valuation.

An architect was required to exclude the value of work from an interim certificate which was not properly executed. If the work was defective and unacceptable as it stood, it had to be classified as work not properly executed until the defect had been remedied.

In carrying out his certification function, the architect is primarily acting for the protection of the employer's interests by determining what payment he can properly make on account. Accordingly, the architect owes the employer a duty to take reasonable care in certifying payments as due.

George Hawkins v Chrysler (1986)

Ordinarily a professional's contractual obligation to his client only extends to agreeing to conduct his services with reasonable skill and care. In the absence of special circumstances, it is not open to the court to extend the normal obligations of a professional beyond the obligation to take reasonable care. In particular, the Court of Appeal rejected the attempt to make the engineer liable for the fitness of purpose obligation. Similarly, the implication of a fitness for purpose obligation in an architect's retainer is highly unusual if the architect is supplying only professional advice or designs. The position may be different if, on the facts of a particular case, the construction professional has agreed to 'design and build' responsibilities for the project or has otherwise taken to have agreed to assume the higher standard of care/warranty.

- Where the facts allow, other terms may be implied such as that the contract administrator will carry out his duties so as to enable the contractor to achieve his contract programme.

10.4 DUTIES OF CARE OWED TO THIRD PARTIES

Contractual duties will only be owed to the client (subject to any collateral warranties, assignment or possibly express reference to others' interests by operation of the *Contracts (Rights of Third Parties) Act* 1999). A duty of care in tort may be owed by a contract administrator to third parties who are not signatories to the contract. In determining to whom such a duty is owed, a distinction must be drawn between pure economic losses and physical damage/personal injury sustained by third parties. Pure economic loss is irrecoverable in tort in the absence of a special relationship of proximity and/or an assumption of responsibility coupled with reasonable reliance, save where such loss is consequential upon *physical* damage in respect of which a relevant duty is owed (see *Murphy v Brentwood* (1991) and *Hedley Byrne v Heller* (1964). However, a contract administrator may be liable to a third party in respect of personal injury or damage caused to a third party or its 'other' property.

10.4.1 Physical damage

AC Billings & Sons Ltd v Riden (1958)

A contractor owed a duty of care in tort to all persons who might be expected to visit the property they were working on to take such care as was, in all the circumstances, reasonable to ensure that they were not exposed to danger. In this particular case, advice that visitors should use a potentially unsafe means of entry to the property whilst the works were in progress was held to be negligent. A mere warning was held to be insufficient to discharge the contractor's duty (although it may lead to a finding of contributory negligence) because of the absence of a suitably safe alternative point of entry to the property.

The position is likely to be the same if a contract administrator gave similar advice.

The contract administrator may well undertake contractual responsibility for applying or supervising the application of health and safety regulations, which would extend his responsibility in this area but is beyond the scope of this book.

Targett v Torfaen Borough Council (1992)

A landlord who is responsible for the design and construction of a house let by him is under a duty to take reasonable care to ensure that the house is free from defects which are likely to cause injury to any person whom he ought reasonably to have in contemplation as likely to be affected by such defects. Such liability was owed by the local authority landlord to a tenant who was injured by falling down dangerously constructed steps.

It was not enough for the landlord to point to the fact that the tenant knew of the danger, in circumstances where it was not realistically possible for the tenant to avoid the danger. Whether knowledge of or an opportunity to inspect a danger is enough to negative a duty of care depends on all the circumstances and whether it is fair, just and reasonable to expect the claimant to remove or avoid the danger.

Clayton v Woodman (1962)

The Court of Appeal considered the extent to which the architect owes a duty of care to a building contractor. Building contractors contracted with a hospital board under an RIBA contract to install a new lift shaft at a hospital. The work was to be supervised by the architects but it was the builders' job to design the manner in which the works were to be carried out and to make all necessary provisions for shoring-up the building during the work.

The architect was asked by the building contractor to consider varying the works to include the demolition of an existing wall. The architect rejected the request. The wall later collapsed, seriously injuring the contractor.

The Court of Appeal rejected the suggestion that the architect was liable in negligence to the builder. The architect would have been in breach of his duty to the employer if he had decided to approve the demolition of the existing wall. The architect did not instruct the builder to do anything he knew to be dangerous. It was a matter for the contractor to determine a safe way of carrying out the works.

The position would have been different if the architect had usurped the role of the contractor and given instructions as to how to carry out the works (rather than merely rejecting a request for a variation).

10.4.2 Economic loss

Jarvis & Sons Ltd v Castle Wharf Developments Ltd (2001)

In this case, a quantity surveyor was held to owe a duty of care to potential contractors who relied upon his representations.

Whilst it remains theoretically possible for a third party purchaser to establish a duty of care situation entitling it to recover pure economic loss from a negligent designer of a building, it is very difficult to conceive of a situation in which the requisite assumption of responsibility and concomitant reliance could actually be established or would be acceptable to a court on policy grounds. A duty of care owed by a contract administrator to a third party outside of any contractual relationship will depend upon the application of the assumption of responsibility / special relationship / reliance test (see *Hedley Byrne* above).

Baxall Securities v Sheard Walshaw Partnership (2002)

The defendant architects were held to owe a limited liability to a subsequent purchaser of commercial property in tort, notwithstanding the absence of a contractual relationship. The duty was owed in respect of damage caused by a latent design defect to property other than the defective item of work itself.

The defendants had been employed on the RIBA conditions to design and supervise the construction of a warehouse between 1989 and 1992 and had issued a final certificate to the contractor in December 1992. The detailed design of the roof drainage was carried out by a specialist subcontractor. The claimants subsequently occupied the warehouse. In 1995 two floods penetrated the roof of the building and damaged the claimant's goods. The floods were caused by the inability of the drainage system to cope with heavy rainfall.

The claimants brought an action in tort against the defendants, alleging that they had negligently failed to design the drainage system to cope with anticipated rainfall. The defendants denied negligence and denied that they owed a duty of care to the claimants as subsequent occupiers of the affected building rather than the client who had engaged the architects.

On appeal the claim failed because the cause of the two floods was found to be a patent defect (the absence of overflows) which should have been spotted by the claimants' surveyors. The claimants' failure to identify the defect broke the chain of causation between the defendants' negligent design and the damage suffered.

As to the duty owed by an architect to a subsequent owner or occupier, the court held that (save where the claim rested on the kind of liability found in *Hedley Byrne v Heller*), there was only a limited duty:

1   First, the duty must be owed in respect of property other than that which is the subject of the design.
2   Secondly, a duty is only owed in relation to damage consequent upon an undiscoverable defect, i.e. a latent defect.

J Jarvis & Sons Ltd v (1) Castle Wharf Developments Ltd (2) Gleeds Management Services Ltd (3) Franklin Ellis Architects Ltd (2001)

A dispute arose out of building works carried out for design and construction works. The first defendant, Castle Wharf, was created for the sole purpose of developing a site. The second defendants, Gleeds, a company of quantity surveyors, were instructed to be agents of the first defendants. Their role included passing information between the first defendants and contractors. The claimant tendered for the design and construction of a phase of the development. The tender was accepted. It later transpired that the first, second and third defendants had not obtained the requisite planning permissions for the works. The claimant commenced proceedings against the defendants on the basis that he had been induced to tender and carry out the construction works by the second defendant's misrepresentations.

The Court of Appeal considered whether a professional agent, such as the second defendant, could be liable to the contractor for his negligent misstatements. It held that:

1   a professional agent of an employer could be liable for a negligent misstatement made to a contractor, where the misrepresentation induces the contractor to tender for the contractor and to rely upon the misstatement;

2   an employer will not be liable for an agent's misrepresentations if he has no independent liability from the agent.

Architype Projects Ltd v Dewhurst Macfarlane & Partners (2004)

It was not arguable that it was fair and reasonable to impose on a subcontractor a duty of care in tort to avoid causing economic loss to an employer. The contractual chain of liability precluded the existence of a tortious relationship.

10.4.3 Summary

- A duty of care in tort may be owed by a contract administrator to third parties who are not signatories to the contract.

- In determining to whom such a duty is owed, a distinction must be drawn between pure economic losses and physical damage/personal injury sustained by third parties.

- Pure economic loss is generally irrecoverable in tort in the absence of a special relationship of proximity and/or an assumption of responsibility coupled with reasonable reliance, save where such loss is consequential upon physical damage in respect of which a relevant duty is owed.

- A contract administrator may be liable to a third party in respect of personal injury or damage caused to a third party or its 'other' property.

10.5 EFFECT OF CONTRACTUAL TERMS ON DUTY OF CARE

Southern Water Authority v Lewis and Duvivier (1985)

The terms of a contract can define and circumscribe the area of risk (in both tort and contract) which a contracting party chooses to accept at common law.

This case concerned the effect of the issue of a taking over-certificate on the liability of subcontractors in respect of the construction of a sewage works. The claimant authority had engaged the main contractor under the Institution of Mechanical Engineers' General Conditions of Contract, Model A form. Those conditions included provisions that:

- the taking-over certificate was not to operate as an admission that the works had been completed in every respect;
- the contractor's liability for making good defects and maintaining the works would be in lieu of any condition or warranty implied by law as to the quality or fitness for purpose of the works taken over under clause 28.

After considering a number of preliminary issues, the court held that:

- the subcontractors could not contractually obtain the benefit of the exclusion of liability in the main contract because they were not signatories to that contract nor had the main contractor entered into it as the subcontractor's agent;
- the subcontractors did owe a duty of care to the claimant authority, but the effect of the taking-over certificate issued by the engineers was to exclude the subcontractors' liability in tort.

Technotrade Ltd v Larkstore Ltd (2006)

Of course, if the contract allows, a party may find that his contractual rights and obligations have been assigned by the original employer to another party. This case found that in circumstances where the cause of action had been transferred but the loss had not, the party to whom the rights of action had been assigned could still recover substantial damages.

The defendant surveying company were unsuccessful in their appeal against a finding of liability in respect of breach of contract in connection with an inadequate site report which they produced for a proposed residential development. The defendant's report was provided pursuant to a contract with the original owner of the development who had subsequently sold the land to the claimant prior to the start of construction. During the construction works a landslip occurred which damaged some of the properties being constructed. The original owner then assigned to the claimant its rights and benefits under the report.

It was held at first instance and on appeal that the claimant, as the assignee of the original cause of action for breach of contract, could bring a claim for substantial damages in respect of the losses caused by the landslip against the defendant.

The court reasoned that the assignment had transferred the cause of action that the original owner had the benefit of (including any remedy in damages), although it had not transferred the loss itself which had been suffered before the assignment when the landslip occurred. The remedy of damages for a breach of contract was not to be limited as a matter of principle to the loss sustained as at the date of the breach of contract or at any particular time thereafter. Further, it was held that the principle that an assignee could not recover more than his assignor should not apply on the facts of the case as it was not intended to permit the contract breaker to avoid all liability by placing the loss that had been sustained into a legal black hole.

10.5.1 Summary

- Where there are concurrent duties owed in both contract and tort, the terms of the contract may circumscribe the nature and extent of the duty owed in tort.

10.6 STATUTORY PROVISIONS EXTENDING DUTIES OWED TO THIRD PARTIES

10.6.1 *Defective Premises Act* 1972

This Act imposes duties upon persons who undertake work for or in connection with the provision of a dwelling after 1 January 1974. The duties are additional to any duty otherwise owed and cannot be excluded or restricted by an undertaking or a contractual term.

Section 1(1) of the Act provides:

'A person taking on work for or in connection with the provision of a dwelling (whether the dwelling is provided by the erection or by the conversion or enlargement of a building) owes a duty –

(a) if the dwelling is provided to the order of any person, to that person; and

(b) without prejudice to paragraph (a) above, to every person who acquires an interest (whether legal or equitable) in the dwelling;

to see that the work which he takes on is done in a workmanlike or, as the case may be, professional manner, with proper materials and so that as regards that work the dwelling will be fit for habitation when completed.'

Thompson v Clive Alexander & Partners (1992)

The plaintiffs owned three houses which had been built to the design of the defendants, who were architects and engineers. The defendants also supervised the works. The plaintiffs alleged that the houses were defective and issued proceedings claiming damages for breach of statutory duty by the defendants pursuant to section 1(1) of the *Defective Premises Act* 1972.

The judge held that the threshold of the duty imposed by the Act is relatively low in that the requirement is to make the building fit for habitation. This means that there is no duty owed under the Act in respect for relatively minor defects that do not make the property uninhabitable.

The Act affords a defence to a contractor or professional consultant who carries out his work in accordance with the express instructions of another (e.g. the employer), so long as he discharges a duty to warn that the instructions being given are defective.

Section 1(2) and (3) provide:

'(2) A person who takes on any such work for another on terms that he is to do it in accordance with instructions given by or on behalf of that other shall, to the extent to which he does it properly in accordance with those instructions, be treated for the purposes of this section as discharging the duty imposed on him by subsection (1) above except where he owes a duty to that other to warn him of any defects in the instructions and fails to discharge that duty.

(3) A person shall not be treated for the purposes of subsection (2) above as having given instructions for the doing of work merely because he has agreed to the work being done in a specified manner, with specified materials or to a specified design.'

10.6.2 *Contracts (Rights of Third Parties) Act 1999*

This Act provides a general and wide-ranging exception to the rule that a party cannot take the benefit of a contract (for instance, by suing for breach of its terms) if he is not a party to it. Section 1(1) provides that a person who is not a party to a contract may nevertheless enforce a term of that contract if either the contract expressly provides that he may do so or if the term purports to confer a benefit on him.

However, instances of successful actions in reliance on the provisions of this Act are very rare because there is no bar to excluding its effect by an express term of the contract. Accordingly, most standard form and bespoke contracts choose to exclude the operation of the Act to prevent third parties acquiring rights under them.

10.6.3 *Compensation Act* 2006

This area of the law has recently been augmented by the *Compensation Act* 2006. Section 1 provides:

> 'A court considering a claim in negligence or breach of statutory duty may, in determining whether the defendant should have taken particular steps to meet a standard of care (whether by taking precautions against a risk or otherwise), have regard to whether a requirement to take those steps might –
>
> (a) prevent a desirable activity from being undertaken at all, to a particular extent or in a particular way; or
>
> (b) discourage persons from undertaking functions in connection with a desirable activity.'

It remains to be seen how the courts will apply this provision and it may be that it goes no further than the requirement that it must be fair, just and reasonable to impose a duty of care to avoid causing economic loss to another person.

The purpose of the Act is to prevent the deterrence of worthwhile activities which might result from a disproportionate fear of litigation. For instance, the Act might be prayed in aid by a school or teacher being sued for negligence for failing to prevent injury befalling a pupil whilst on a school trip. In the construction field, it is conceivable that the Act might be a relevant consideration where a particularly fraught analysis of the fair, just and reasonable test must be made or where the works themselves are particularly noble or worthwhile.

10.6.4 Summary

- The *Defective Premises Act* 1972 creates a duty owed by persons who undertake work for or in connection with the provision of a dwelling to a subsequent occupier of that property to ensure that it is habitable, notwithstanding the absence of a contractual or other relationship between them.

- Under the *Contracts (Rights of Third Parties) Act* 1999, a person who is not a party to a contract may nevertheless enforce a term of that contract if the contract either expressly provides that he may do so or it purports to confer a benefit on him.

- The *Compensation Act* 2006 may make a finding of a duty of care owed to a third party less likely if the defendant was carrying out a desirable activity when the alleged breach of duty occurred.

10.7 CONTRIBUTION

Under the *Law Reform (Contributory Negligence) Act* 1945, section 1(1), liability may be apportioned between claimant and defendant where the claimant's own negligence has contributed to the his damage in the following circumstances:

> 'Where any person suffers damage as the result partly of his own fault and partly of the fault of any other person or persons, a claim in respect of that damage shall not be defeated by reason of the fault of the person suffering the damage, but the damages recoverable in respect thereof shall be reduced to such extent as the court thinks just and equitable having regard to the claimant's share in the responsibility for the damage.'

Barclays Bank plc v Fairclough Building Ltd (1995)

The plaintiff employer issued proceedings to recover damages for breaches by the defendant contractor of two principal obligations contained in a standard form of building contract (the JCT standard form (1984 edition)). Both clauses required strict performance and did not depend on a mere failure to take reasonable care.

The trial judge at first instance found that the contractor was liable but that the employer's architect had failed to supervise the work so as to prevent the contractor from committing that fault. The judge gave judgment for the employer for damages to be assessed but, on the basis of the above section of the *Law Reform (Contributory Negligence) Act* 1945 held that such damages should be reduced by 40 per cent for contributory negligence by the employer's architect.

However, this decision was reversed on appeal. Although a defendant contractor was entitled to the benefit of apportionment of blame and liability under section 1(1) of the 1945 Act, if the liability for the breach was the same as, and coextensive with, a similar liability in tort independent of the existence of the contract on a claim for damages founded on a breach by the contractor of a strict contractual liability that arose independently of any negligence on his part, the contract had to be construed so as to exclude the operation of section 1(1) of the 1945 Act. There was no express obligation on the employer to prevent breaches being committed by the contractor and accordingly the employer could recover its damages in full.

Royal Brompton Hospital Trust v Hammond and others (2002)

The House of Lords considered the proper interpretation of the statute that allows the courts to apportion liability between different defendants who were found liable to the same claimant. Their Lordships applied a restrictive construction to section 1(1) of the *Civil Liability (Contribution) Act* 1978 which on the face of it allowed a defendant to claim a contribution from a third party who was wholly or partially liable to the claimant for the same damaged being claimed against him.

Section 1(1) provides:

'Subject to the following provisions of this section, any person liable in respect of any damage suffered by another person may recover contribution from any other person liable in respect of the same damage (whether jointly with him or otherwise).'

The employer alleged that the architect was negligent in that he should have known that the contractor was not entitled to an architect's instruction to lay a moisture resistant membrane and the employer sought to recover damages from the architect. The employer claimed (1) sums paid to the contractor in respect of and consequential on the instruction; (2) the recovery of liquidated damages paid to the contractor upon the instruction; and/or (3) any other sums paid to the contractor in consequence of the instruction, extensions of time and/or prolongation. The employer said it was entitled to these sums because they were the *same damage* for the purposes of the section 1(1) of the *Contribution Act* as set out above.

In its defence, the architect denied that it was negligent. In the alternative, it said that if it was negligent in granting the extensions of time to the contractor, then the contractor was also liable to the employer in respect of the same damage which was the subject matter of the action against the architect and thus was liable to contribute to the extent of a complete indemnity for such loss as the architect may be held liable to the employer pursuant to the same provision of the *Contribution Act* as the employer relied on.

Their Lordships held that *'same damage'* could not be given a wide interpretation such that it meant 'substantially or materially the same damage'. It had to be exactly the same. Accordingly, when a claim for contribution arises the questions to be asked are: (i) What damage had Party A suffered? (ii) Was Party B liable in respect of that damage? and (iii) Was Party C also liable to A in respect of that damage or some of it?

In the circumstances, both claims for contribution (i.e. by the contractor and the architect) failed because they were not for the same damage. The employer's claim against the contractor was for late delivery of the building, while the essence of the case against the architects was that their breach of duty had changed detrimentally the employer's contractual position against the contractor.

Baker & Davies plc v Leslie Wilks Associates (2006)

The claimant building contractors engaged the defendant engineers to monitor a property for cracking. The engineers failed to report the full extent of the problem and it was not in fact discovered for a further two years. Any claims the employer may have had against the building contractors were settled by the payment of money and an agreement that the contractor would carry out remedial works at its own cost.

The contractor then pursued the engineers for a contribution. Section 1(4) of the *Civil Liability (Contribution) Act* 1978 allows a claimant in the contractor's position to recover a contribution in respect of 'any payment in bona fide settlement'. The question faced by the court was whether the contractor could recover the costs it incurred remedying the works itself as part of the settlement agreement. It was held that the word 'payment' is capable of including 'payment in kind', at any rate where that payment is capable of valuation in monetary worth. Accordingly, the contractors' claim could succeed.

Brian Warwicker Partnership v Hok International Ltd (2006)

The court considered the factors relevant to determining the correct apportionment of damages in a contribution claim and confirmed that blameworthiness is a relevant factor to be considered when allocating the amount of a contribution. Such blameworthiness could apparently be considered even if it was not strictly causative of the damage.

10.7.1 Summary

- The court may apportion damages between defendants or between the claimant and defendant in accordance with its view of the respective culpability of the parties for the same damage.

11
Limitation and the duration of a contract administrator's obligations

Typically, the contract administrator's active duties continue past the issue of the certificate of practical completion, through the defects liability period and conclude at the time of the issue of the final certificate. The exact dates of completion will depend on the terms of the contract.

Of course, the issue of the final certificate does not bring to an end the contract administrator's potential liability for damages for breach of his contract and/or his other obligations: if a breach of his obligations does not come to light until later, proceedings may still be brought, notwithstanding the end of the works. However, there are strict timeframes within which proceedings must be issued. The logic behind this is that whilst a party must, in broad terms at least, be prepared to shoulder his fair share of the burden should construction works be defective, he should not hold himself open for an indefinite period of time to answer a 'stale' claim. The timeframes in question have been fixed by Parliament since 1623 and are currently set out in the *Limitation Act* 1980.

11.1 LIMITATION FOR BREACH OF CONTRACT

Limitation Act 1980, section 5, section 8

'1   Time limit for actions founded on simple contract

An action founded on simple contract shall not be brought after the expiration of six years from the date on which the cause of action accrued.

2　Time limits for actions on a specialty [including a contract under seal]

An action upon a specialty shall not be brought after the expiration of twelve years from the date on which the cause of action accrued.

Subsection (1) above shall not affect any action for which a shorter period of limitation is prescribed by any other provision of this Act.'

11.1.1 Cause of action is usually breach of contract

Gibbs v Guild (1881)

That a party's cause of action will accrue at the time of breach of contract is a long-standing principle of English law which dates back to the beginning of contract law. It is the breach of contract which is the 'gist of the action'; consequently, time will run from the date of such a breach.

Bagot v Stevens Scanlon & Co. (1964)

The plaintiff owner employed the defendant architect to supervise the construction of a drainage system, pursuant to a standard form building contract, entered into in March 1955. The defendant architects continued their supervision until February 1957. In the latter part of 1961, several of the pipes in the drainage system broke or cracked. On 2 April 1963 the plaintiff commenced proceedings against the defendant for breach of contractual duty to supervise the works properly.

The issue was the whether the action for negligence against the architect for negligent supervision ran from the date of the last act of negligence or the date when the damage first occurred. The supervision ended more than six years before the writ was issued. The damage (to drainage pipes) became apparent four years after the supervisory duties came to an end, albeit that arguably the damage itself occurred when the drains were constructed.

Held: The answer depended on whether the action arose in contract, tort or both. The duty to exercise reasonable skill and care where the failure was to do the very thing contracted to be done, arose out of contract alone and, in cases of professional relationships, such a duty did not arise also independently of contract; accordingly, the action was statute barred.

Lancashire and Cheshire Association of Baptist Churches Inc v Howard & Seddon Partnership (a firm) (1993)

The defendant architect was responsible for the design of a sanctuary and supervision of associated building works. It later transpired that the sanctuary was not satisfactory, suffering from poor ventilation and condensation problems. By a writ dated 11 December 1986, the plaintiff brought an action against the defendant for breach of contract and/or breach of duty of care. At a preliminary hearing it was held that the claim for breach of contract was statute-barred. The defendant architect contended that because a contractual relationship existed between the parties there could not, as a matter of law, be a concurrent duty in tort.

Kershaw J held that where a contractual relationship exists between the parties, a concurrent duty can exist in tort.

New Islington and Hackney Housing Association Limited v Pollard Thomas and Edwards Limited (2001)

The defendants were appointed in 1990 as architects in respect of the design and construction of six properties on various sites acquired by the claimant housing authority. Soon after the works were practically complete (February–March 1992) and the properties occupied, the claimant became aware of numerous complaints from residents concerning noise. The claimant brought proceedings on 1 May 1998 for breach of contract and negligence, claiming that the defendants' design failed to incorporate adequate soundproofing between flats.

Dyson J held that upon a proper construction of the contract and of the defendants' terms and conditions of engagement, it could not be said that the defendants were under a duty to review the adequacy of design (in particular the adequacy sound insulation) after practical completion had taken place. Consequently, breach took place before 1 May 1992, and proceedings were dismissed.

11.1.2 Summary

- The ordinary time-limit in which a party must bring a claim is six years from the date of breach of the contract.
- If a contract is under seal, then the time-limit will be 12 years from date of its breach.
- It may be that a specific term of a contract warrants or guarantees the durability of the goods or works in question for a period beyond the time limits laid down by statute. In such circumstances, an action for breach of warranty may properly be brought outside statutory time limits.
- The position is different where defects have been deliberately concealed. This is discussed below.

11.2 LIMITATION FOR BREACH OF STATUTORY DUTY

Some statutes that create rights and obligations also provide their own limitation period that shall apply to those rights and obligations.

Defective Premises Act 1972, section 1(5)

Section 1(5) of this Act provides:

'1(5) Any cause of action in respect of a breach of the duty imposed by this section shall be deemed ... to have accrued at a time when the dwelling was completed, but if after that time a person who has done work for or in connection with the provision of the dwelling does further work to rectify the work he has already done, any such cause of action in respect of that further work shall be deemed for those purposes to have accrued at the time when the further work was finished.'

Alderson v Beetham Organization Ltd (2003)

The defendants were property developers who were responsible for converting a building into flats in 1994. The claimant purchased a long leasehold interest in one of the flats in 1995. Soon after occupation it was discovered that the flat was susceptible to damp. Remedial works, consisting of the re-laying of floor slabs and the fitting of extra drainage, were undertaken by the defendants in 1995 but were ineffective. It transpired that this was because the root cause of the problems was the failure of the Newton damp-proofing system. The claimant brought an action under the *Defective Premises Act* 1972) in 2001, claiming that the defendants had breached their statutory duty to render the property fit for human habitation. The defendants argued that the claim was statute-barred: whilst a new cause of action accrued in 1995 in respect of the remedial works (i.e. the floor slabs and extra drainage), no new cause of action in respect of the original works (i.e. the damp-proofing) arose.

The Court of Appeal rejected the defendant's contentions, and held that in cases where a party has come back to repair a defect but failed to repair it properly, a fresh cause of action accrues at the time of the failed remedial works. In the circumstances, the claim was allowed.

11.2.1 Contribution

The *Limitation Act* 1980 provides a special limitation period for claims for a contribution. The relevant parts of section 10 of the Act provide:

'10(1) Where under section 1 of the Civil Liability (Contribution) Act 1978 any person becomes entitled to a right to recover contribution in respect of any damage from any other person, no action to recover contribution by virtue of that right shall be brought after the expiration of two years from the date on which that right accrued.

(2) For the purposes of this section the date on which a right to recover contribution in respect of any damage accrues to any person (referred to below in this section as 'the relevant date') shall be ascertained as provided in subsections (3) and (4) below.

(3) If the person in question is held liable in respect of that damage –

(a) by a judgment given in any civil proceedings; or

(b) by an award made on any arbitration;

the relevant date shall be the date on which the judgment is given or the date of the award (as the case may be).

For the purposes of this subsection no account shall be taken of any judgment or award given or made on appeal in so far as it varies the amount of damages awarded against the person in question.

(4) If, in any case not within subsection (3) above, the person in question makes or agrees to make any payment to one or more persons in compensation for that damage (whether he admits any liability in respect of the damage or not), the relevant date shall be the earliest date on which the amount to be paid by him is agreed between him (or his representative) and the person (or each of the persons as the case may be) to whom the payment is to be made.'

Aer Lingus v Gildacroft Ltd (2006)

The Court of Appeal considered how section 10(3) of the *Limitation Act* 1980 (above) applied where the judgment in question had been split between liability and quantum and handed down on different dates. The court held that it was the later, quantum judgment that started time running for these purposes.

11.2.2 Summary

- Limitation under the *Defective Premises Act* 1972 runs from the time that the dwelling (or further work carried out to it by the defendant) was completed.

- The time limit in which claims may be brought under the *Civil Liability (Contribution) Act* 1978 is two years from the date of the judgment, award or settlement agreement in respect of which a contribution is claimed.

11.3 LIMITATION IN TORT

Limitation Act 1980, section 2
'2. Time limits for actions founded on tort

An action founded on tort shall not be brought after the expiration of six years from the date on which the cause of action accrued.'

11.3.1 Cause of action accrues on the date that damage occurs

Pirelli General Cable Works Limited v Oscar Faber & Partners (1983)

The defendant consulting engineers were employed by the claimant to advise on the design of a chimney which was subsequently built in 1969. It transpired that the design was defective in that it provided for inappropriate materials to be incorporated into the structure, and expert evidence determined that cracking, which was not actually discovered until 1977, manifested itself no later than 1970. With reasonable diligence, the claimant could have been expected to have discovered the cracking in 1972. Proceedings were issued in 1978; the defendant contended the same were time-barred.

The House of Lords held that a cause of action in tort accrues on the date of the damage itself, not from the date upon when such damage was discovered or ought reasonably to have been discovered. Consequently, the claimant's case was time-barred as the writ was served more than six years after 1970.

Abbott v Will Gannon and Smith Ltd (2005)

Design work to a hotel by the defendant structural engineers was completed in March 1997. Cracking had occurred by late 1999 and a claim was issued for breach of contract and negligence in September 2003.

The contract claim was agreed to be statute-barred, but the first instance judge held that if cracks appeared within six years of the issue of proceedings, the claim is not statute-barred in tort. The Court of Appeal upheld the decision and affirmed that the starting position for the limitation period in tort claims for defective construction is as set out in *Pirelli v Oscar Faber* (above).

11.3.2 Establishing the 'date of damage'

Pirelli remains the leading authority on limitation in actions brought in tort. It is also remembered for the dictum of Lord Fraser, who mooted the confusing concept that, in some circumstances, the date of damage might well occur upon completion of a building if it is so manifestly defective that it is 'doomed from the start' (at 16, 18):

> 'There may perhaps be cases where the defect is so gross that the building is doomed from the start, and where the owner's cause of action will accrue as soon as it is built, but it seems unlikely that such a defect would not be discovered within the limitation period. Such cases, if they exist, would be exceptional.
>
> ... except perhaps where the advice of an architect or consulting engineer leads to the erection of a building which is so defective as to be doomed from the start, the cause of action arises only when physical damage occurs to the building.'

Ketteman v Hansel Properties Limited (1985) 1 All ER 352

In 1975 the claimant homeowners purchased houses built by the defendant builders. The following year, cracking occurred which was discovered to be attributable to settlement of the foundations, which had been laid pursuant to an architect's designs between 1973 and 1975. Rather than suffer the inconvenience of underpinning works, the claimants decided to sell their properties at a loss. The architect was joined as a defendant in 1982 when the financial viability of the defendant builders was called into question.

The architect sought to argue that the claim against it was out of time on the grounds that the houses were 'doomed from the start': the plans and siting being faulty, the foundations were bound to settle and cause damage.

The Court of Appeal rejected this argument, following *Pirelli* and holding that the cause of action accrued on the date of the cracking (i.e. in 1976). Only in very exceptional cases will a building be 'doomed from the start'. Consequently, the proceedings were brought in time.

London Congregational Union v Harriss & Harriss (1988)

The defendant, a firm of architects, was retained by the claimant to design and oversee building works to construct a new church hall. During the course of such works, the contractor omitted to fit a damp-proof course, an omission which was not picked up on by the defendant. Final completion occurred in 1970. Between 1971 and 1975 the building flooded on several occasions as a result of defectively designed drains, and further damage was caused to the blockwork of the hall from water ingress a result of the missing damp-proof course. Proceedings were issued against the defendant in 1978. The defendant argued that the cause of action accrued at the time of erection and/or practical completion of the building, as: (i) the defective drain design was the 'damage' to the property, or (ii) the property was 'doomed from the start' (see commentary on *Pirelli* above).

The Court of Appeal held that limitation ran from the date that water damage was caused to the building and the claim was not statute-barred. The design of the drains and the missing damp-proof course were examples of defects which, although causative of the water ingress, did not constitute actionable damage in themselves. The court suggested that there may be circumstances where a defect could constitute actual physical damage to the building, but only where such defects were immediately causative of damage. Even if such damage was inevitable, this is still not sufficient to ground a cause of action. In the circumstances, the drains had been functional for almost two years.

Nitrigin Eireann Teoranta v Inco Alloys Ltd (1992)

This case concerned an explosion in a chemical plant following the escape of methane gas from a pipe supplied by the defendants. The gas escaped from a crack in a section of pipework in 1984, but the same section had in fact cracked (but was repaired) in 1983. Proceedings were not issued until 1990. The defendants argued that limitation ran from the time of the first incidence of cracking (i.e. in 1983) with the result that the proceedings were time-barred.

The court held that the first incidence of cracking, being damage to the pipe itself, constituted 'pure economic loss' (as opposed to damage to 'other' property) and thus no cause of action arose. However, the later incidence of cracking was causative of physical damage to 'other' property (i.e. to the plant surrounding the pipe), and a cause of action first accrued when this actionable damage occurred. Consequently, proceedings had been brought in time.

Nykredit Mortgage Bank plc v Edward Erdman Group Ltd (1997)

On the strength of a valuation report supplied by the defendant, the claimant bank agreed to advance £2.45m to a borrower in respect of a property. The defendants represented that the value of the property was in the region of £3.5m. In actual fact, it transpired that the true value of the property at the time of the valuation was closer to £2m.

The claimant argued that had it been made aware of this at the time, it would not have agreed to advance such a high sum to the borrower, who in the meantime had defaulted on mortgage repayments, obliging the claimants to take possession of the property and sell it. The price achieved at sale was £345,000. The claimant issued proceedings against the defendant in both contract and tort.

The House of Lords held that a cause of action accrued when the claimant first sustained 'measurable relevant loss'. This was deemed to be at or around the time the mortgage was granted. The bank suffered actual loss almost immediately as the borrower had defaulted straight away on repayments and, further, at all times the bank's loan had exceeded the true value of the property.

Havenledge Ltd v Graeme John & Partners (2000)

This case illustrates the difficulty the courts have had in establishing the 'date of damage'. Whilst there was no dispute that the relevant test to apply was when the injured party suffer actual (as opposed to potential or prospective) loss or damage of a kind recognised by law, all three judges arrived at different conclusions as to when such loss was suffered. By a majority of two-to-one, the claim was allowed to proceed.

The claimants purchased a property in 1987 for the purposes of refurbishing and converting the same into a nursing home. The defendants were a firm of solicitors who negligently failed to advise the claimants to obtain a mining engineer's report in respect of the property prior to purchase.

Over the next five years, mining operations were carried out within influencing distance of the property. Cracks began to appear prior to February 1990 but were not discovered until August 1990. Extensive remedial works were undertaken between 1990 and 1994 and paid for by British Coal.

The claimants alleged that following the discovery of the cracks in August 1990, the nursing home ceased to be a viable business concern and was forced to close down. The claimants brought proceedings in February 1996 to recover losses incurred as a result of the business going into receivership.

Sir Anthony Evans held that the 'relevant loss' was the lost business investment and the financial consequences of the disruption to the business. On the facts, this was not suffered until the date of the discovery of the cracks in August 1990, as it was from such discovery that interference to the business began. Consequently, proceedings were issued in time.

Pill LJ held that it was the expenditure of sums on the conversion of the property into a nursing home which was the relevant loss in this case. That expenditure (which was, of course, part of the business investment) was 'abortive' as the property was unsuitable for use as a nursing home. Time ran from when such monies were first spent, which was within the limitation period.

Buxton LJ dissented, holding that loss was suffered at the time of the purchase of the building; from that moment, the claimants were burdened with an unsuitable property for their business concerns. As a result, the action was time-barred.

New Islington and Hackney Housing Association Limited v Pollard Homas and Edwards Limited (2001)

The facts of this case (and the position regarding limitation in respect of breach of contract) are set out at 11.1.1 above.

The claimant also brought proceedings against the defendants in tort. However, the result was the same: such proceedings were time-barred. Dyson J held that the claimant's cause of action accrued, at the latest, at the time of practical completion, as the buildings suffered from a lack of adequate sound insulation (and therefore economic loss had been sustained) from the outset.

The grounds upon which Dyson J distinguished *London Congregational Union v Harriss* are important to note:

> 'In *Harriss* , the damaging consequences of the defective drains were not immediately effective, since the drains were capable of functioning properly as drains, and did so function, for 20 months. Accordingly the physical damage was not suffered until those damaging consequences first occurred. In the present case, the sound insulation was inadequate from the date of handover. It was never capable of being fit for the purpose. In the language of "damaging consequences", those consequences were immediately effective. From the outset, the building suffered from lack of adequate sound insulation. It is the building that suffers from the defect, and that is what is required to enable the owner to complete his cause of action in negligence.'

Tesco v Costain Construction Ltd (2004)

The defendant building contractors were engaged by the claimant to design and build a new superstore. Practical completion occurred in 1990, but the building was subsequently damaged by a catastrophic fire which broke out in 2001. The claimant alleged that the defendant was negligent and/or in breach of contract for failing to install appropriate fire stopping measures.

The court held that the claimant's cause of action in tort accrued upon completion of the building: the store was less valuable from that moment onwards than it would have been had the fire inhibiting measures been incorporated into it. In other words, given that a 'special relationship' was held to exist between the parties (by virtue of the underlying contract, if nothing else), the claimant suffered actionable damage in the form of 'pure economic loss' from the outset, and not from the date of the fire.

The judge distinguished *Pirelli* and *London Congregational Union v Harriss* (cases in which the cause of action was held to arise on the date of the physical damage, not completion of the works) on the basis that the nature of the deficiency in question was the 'lack of a desirable attribute' (i.e. more extensive fire stopping) rendering the building less capable of resisting fire damage, as opposed to the use of unsuitable materials which made physical damage inevitable.

Abbott v Will Gannon & Smith Limited (2005)

This case is also considered at 11.3. The defendants were structural engineers who were engaged in 1995 by the claimant hoteliers to carry out design work to remedy structural defects in a bay window at the claimant's hotel in Torquay. In March 1997, remedial works were completed pursuant to the defendants' designs. Two years later, in 1999, the bay window suffered further damage, necessitating further remedial works at a cost of £20,000. The claimants issued proceedings in both contract and tort in September 2003, although subsequently conceded that the claim in contract was time-barred.

The defendants sought to argue that the property was defective upon completion of the initial remedial works, the claimants suffered economic loss upon this date as the bay window was defective. The Court of Appeal rejected this argument and followed *Pirelli* , leaving it to the House of Lords to decide whether *Pirelli* was 'still the law' or not. The loss occurred at the time that physical damage occurred to the window in 1999.

Mummery LJ, delivering the leading judgment, went on to rule that if the Court of Appeal was bound by *Pirelli* , then any 'economic loss' was not in fact sustained by the claimant until 1999. This was the date when the defective design works manifested themselves in such a way that the value of the building was affected.

11.3.3 Summary

- In tort, limitation runs from the 'date of damage'.
- It is not always straightforward to establish when such 'damage' occurs.
- To be actionable, the damage complained of must be a 'measurable relevant loss'. Potential, or even inevitable, damage is not sufficient.

- What constitutes a 'measurable relevant loss' will depend heavily on the facts in every case.

- It seems that the type of loss claimed will dictate when the 'relevant damage' occurs. Thus a cause of action may arise after physical damage manifests itself in the building.

- In some circumstances, damage will be suffered from the outset. This will inevitably take the form of 'pure economic loss'. The authors are not aware of any cases in which the 'doomed from the start' scenario has been successfully argued.

- Following *Abbott v Gannon*, it may be the case that 'pure economic loss' is not actually suffered for the purposes of triggering limitation until the defect in question manifests itself so as to affect the value of the building.

- Where the defect in question is flawed design or construction which renders physical damage inevitable (as opposed to a defect which is simply the lack of a 'desirable attribute' (such as sound insulation or fire stopping)), then it appears that limitation will run from when such physical damage occurs.

11.4 *LATENT DAMAGE ACT* 1986

Where damage resulting from an act of negligence is not discoverable until after it actually occurs, a claimant may derive assistance from the provisions of the *Latent Damage Act* 1986 which operate so as to extend the limitation period in which to bring an action.

Essentially, the *Latent Damage Act* 1986 inserts additional sections into the *Limitation Act* 1980 (specifically, for our purposes sections 14A, 14B and 32(5)), but applies to actions in negligence; it will not apply to a claim brought only in contract (see *JK Buckingham v Iron Trades Mutual Insurance* (1990)).

11.4.1 Extension of limitation period

Limitation Act 1980, sections 14A and 14B

'**14A Special time limit for negligence actions where facts relevant to cause of action are not known at date of accrual**

(1) This section applies to any action for damages for negligence, other than one to which section 11 of this Act applies [personal injury], where the starting date for reckoning the period of limitation under subsection 4(b) below falls after the date on which the cause of action accrued.

(2) Section 2 of this Act shall not apply to an action to which this section applies.

(3) An action to which this section applies shall not be brought after the expiration of the period applicable in accordance with subsection (4) below.

(4) That period is either:

(a) six years from the date on which the cause of action accrued; or

(b) three years from the starting date as defined by subsection (5) below, if that period expires later than the period mentioned in paragraph (a) above.

(5) For the purposes of this section, the starting date for reckoning the period of limitation under subsection (4)(b) above is the earliest date on which the plaintiff or any person in whom the cause of action was vested before him first had both the knowledge required for bringing an action for damages in respect of the relevant damage and a right to bring such an action.

(6) In subsection (5) above "the knowledge required for bringing an action for damages in respect of the relevant damage" means knowledge both:

(a) of the material facts about the damage in respect of which damages are claimed; and

(b) of the other facts relevant to the current action mentioned in subsection (8) below.

(7) For the purposes of subsection (6)(a) above, the material facts about the damage are such facts about the

damage as would lead a reasonable person who had suffered such damage to consider it sufficiently serious to justify his instituting proceedings for damages against a defendant who did not dispute liability and was able to satisfy a judgment.

(8) The other facts referred to in subsection (6)(b) above are:

(a) that the damage was attributable in whole or in part to the act or omission which is alleged to constitute negligence; and

(b) the identity of the defendant; and

(c) if it is alleged that the act or omission was that of a person other than the defendant, the identity of that person and the additional facts supporting the bringing of an action against the defendant.

(9) Knowledge that any acts or omissions did or did not, as a matter of law, involve negligence is irrelevant for the purposes of subsection (5) above.

(10) For the purposes of this section a person's knowledge includes knowledge which he might reasonably have been expected to acquire:

(a) from facts observable or ascertainable by him; or

(b) from facts ascertainable by him with the help of appropriate expert advice which it is reasonable for him to seek;

but a person shall not be taken by virtue of this subsection to have knowledge of a fact ascertainable only with the help of expert evidence so long as he has taken all reasonable steps to obtain (and, where appropriate, to act on) that advice.

14B Overriding time limit for negligence actions not involving personal injuries

(1) An action for damages for negligence, other than one to which section 11 of this Act applies, shall not be brought after the expiration of fifteen years from this date (or, if more than one, from the last of the dates) on which there occurred any act or omission:

(a) which is alleged to constitute negligence; and

(b) to which the damage in respect of which damages are claimed is alleged to be attributable (in whole or in part).

(2) This section barred the right of action in a case to which subsection (1) above applies notwithstanding that:

(a) the cause of action has not yet accrued; or

(b) where section 14A of this Act applies to the action, the date which is for the purposes of that section the starting date for reckoning the period mentioned in subsection (4)(b) of that section has not yet occurred;

before the end of the period of limitation prescribed by this section.'

Kensington & Chelsea Area Health Authority v Wettern Composites and others (1984)

This case has been considered at chapter 3 and 6.3.2 and 9.6 above. In an action against architects and consulting engineers, arising from the consequences of defectively fixed stone to Westminster Hospital, the court held that for the purposes of the *Limitation Act* 1980, the damage occurred when substantial movement first affected the stone.

For the purposes of limitation, time starts to run in respect of claims that concern liability for latent defects in tort only when the claimant had both the knowledge required for bringing an action for damages in respect of the relevant damage and a right to bring such an action. Section 14 of the *Latent Damage Act* 1986 provides that, once those two conditions have been fulfilled, the claimant has three years in which to bring his claim.

11.4.2 Summary

- A party's cause of action in negligence will still accrue when damage occurs.
- Pursuant to *Limitation Act* 1980, section 14A, the limitation period for bringing an action in negligence will expire after either six years from when the cause of action accrues (i.e. from the date of the damage itself) or three years from the 'starting date' (often referred to as the 'date of discoverability' of the damage), whichever is the later.

- Pursuant to *Limitation Act* 1980, section 14A(5), the 'starting date' is the earliest date on which the would-be claimant had both the knowledge required for bringing an action for damages in respect of the relevant damage and a right to bring such an action.

- Pursuant to *Limitation Act* 1980, section 14B, in all cases, the limitation period for bringing an action in negligence will expire 15 years after the date of the negligent act.

- The position is different where defects have been deliberately concealed is subject to different rules (as to which, see below).

11.5 CONCEALMENT, MISTAKE AND FRAUD

Limitation Act 1980, section 32

'32 Postponement of limitation period in case of fraud, concealment or mistake

(1) Subject to [subsections (3) and (4A)] below, where in the case of any action for which a period of limitation is prescribed by this Act, either

(a) The action is based upon the fraud of the defendant; or

(b) Any fact relevant to the plaintiff's right of action has been deliberately concealed from him by the defendant; or

(c) The action is for relief from the consequences of a mistake;

the period of limitation shall not begin to run until the plaintiff has discovered the fraud, concealment or mistake (as the case may be) or could with reasonable diligence have discovered it.

References in this subsection to the defendant include references to the defendant's agent and to any person through whom the defendant claims and his agent

(2) For the purposes of subsection (1) above, deliberate commission of a breach of duty in circumstances in which it is unlikely to be discovered for some time amounts to a deliberate concealment of the facts involved in that breach of duty.

(3) Nothing in this section shall enable any action

(a) To recover, or recover the value of, any property; or

(b) To enforce any charge against, or set aside any transaction affecting, any property;

to be brought against the purchaser of the property or any person claiming through him in any case where the property has been purchased for valuable consideration by an innocent third party since the fraud or concealment or (as the case may be) the transaction in which the mistake was made took place.

(4) A purchaser is an innocent third party for the purposes of this section

(a) In the case of fraud or concealment of any fact relevant to the plaintiff's right of action, if he was not a party to the fraud or (as the case may be) to the concealment of that fact and did not at the time of the purchase know or have reason to believe that the fraud or concealment had taken place; and

(b) In the case of mistake, if he did not at the time of the purchase know or have reason to believe that the mistake had been made ...

(5) Sections 14A and 14B of this Act shall not apply to any action to which subsection (1)(b) above applies (and accordingly the period of limitation referred to in that subsection, in any case to which either of those sections would otherwise apply, is the period applicable under section 2 of this Act).'

The practical application of *Limitation Act* 1980, section 32 in the context of building disputes normally arises in circumstances where the defect in question that has caused damage has been deliberately concealed, such concealment constituting fraud for the purposes of the Act.

Should this occur, a party may bring an action against another party within six years from the earliest date when the concealment was discovered or was reasonably discoverable.

This is the position in both claims brought in contract and in negligence (i.e. in respect of the latter, the 15-year longstop provision will not apply).

King v Victor Parsons (1973)

The defendants were estate developers who agreed to construct a semi-detached property for the claimant in 1961. Prior to construction, the defendants took architectural advice and were informed that the site was, up until 1954, used as a rubbish tip. As a result, the architect advised that either reinforced concrete raft foundations or piled foundations connected by reinforced concrete ground beams be dug. The defendants chose to ignore this advice, and construction of the property began without piled or raft foundations. Instead, the builder simply laid down spreading concrete reinforced with a 'makeshift' grillage as an underlay for the floors. In 1968 the claimant was woken at night by a loud crack. Further cracking occurred and subsequent surveys established that the property was uninhabitable and would have to be pulled down. The claimant sued the defendants for damages in 1969.

In holding that the *Limitation Act* 1980 did not apply so as to bar the claimant's claim, the Court of Appeal ruled that in order to establish 'fraud' it was not necessary to show that a party took active steps to conceal his wrongdoing. Rather, it was enough that such wrongdoing was either knowingly done (with nothing said to the other) or recklessly done (like the 'man who turns a blind eye') to conceal the other party's right of action.

However, if on the facts a defendant merely commits an 'honest blunder' then he can avail himself of the statute. It seems that some affectation of conscience is therefore necessary in order to prove deliberate concealment: merely pleading that the defendant 'ought to have known' of his errors is not enough.

London Borough of Lewisham v Leslie (1980)

The claimant was the successor to the London County Council which had engaged the defendant contractors to construct four tower blocks in Lewisham in 1960. Construction works were completed in 1961. During the course of a routine fire inspection in 1971, it was discovered that there was a gap between the concrete shell and the cladding of one of the buildings. Further investigations were carried out and it transpired that the contractor had neglected to fit approximately three-quarters of the required number of Abbey ties to seal the cladding to the concrete shell. Considerable remedial works were required and an action was brought in 1976 against the defendant to recover the costs of the same. The defendant argued that the proceedings were time-barred.

Lewisham relied on the judgment in *King v Victor Parsons* (see above), arguing that the defects had been kept concealed both from itself and its predecessors; accordingly, time did not run against its claim until discovery of the defects in 1971. The Court of Appeal agreed with the claimant.

No distinction should be drawn between small-scale residential works and large, publicly-funded tower blocks: the mere fact that London County Council employed architects and surveyors who may have been in a position to notice any defects as they arose was not automatically sufficient for the defendant to defeat the allegation of deliberate concealment. This will be a matter of fact in each case. As Lord Denning MR explained (at 28):

> 'It only requires a little imagination to think of circumstances in which workmen may do their work badly, leaving defects – which the architect or supervisor would not discover, even by using reasonable diligence … It is all very well to talk about the Council having its own architects and supervisors. But these gentlemen may have been misled by the contractors. The bad work may have been done when they were away or their backs were turned for some good reason.'

Kaliszewska v John Clague & Partners (1984)

The claimant engaged the defendant architect to design a single-storey dwelling-house at a site in Kent. The ground was largely comprised of London clay. Unbeknown to the claimant, the defendant's design was defective in that it did not make proper provisions for settlement and heave conditions which should have been anticipated on the site. In 1974, four years after the house was completed, cracking appeared. The cracks worsened in 1976 and in 1978 an independent expert advised that underpinning was necessary. The claimant brought an action to recover the costs of remedial works in 1982.

The judge ruled that the property was an 'exceptional' case and was satisfied that the building was 'doomed from the start' with some movement damage having in fact occurred at a very early stage (in 1971). The judge further held that the defendant was guilty only of incompetence, and not deliberate concealment, even though in designer had deliberately rejected contemporaneous architectural wisdom as 'idealistic'.

Gray v TP Bennett & Son (1989)

The claimant brought proceedings in 1983 in respect of defective construction works which were carried out in or around 1962 by the fourth defendants, who were responsible for erecting a blockwork fascia to a building, to be tied to the concrete shell by wall ties and reinforced concrete projections (or 'nibs'). Completion of the works was carried out in 1963 with final completion two years later.

When the blockwork fascia began to bow in 1979, investigations revealed that a large proportion of the 'nibs' had been hacked back to overcome problems with alignment, leaving the blockwork in a perilous condition. Proceedings were issued in 1983.

The court held that the fourth defendants had deliberately concealed the 'butchering of the concrete nibs' and that the action was not statute-barred; the hacking was not reasonably discoverable until 1979. Further, the court rejected the argument that the first defendant, a firm of architects, should have discovered the hacking upon a reasonable inspection of the works. In the circumstances, it was not the architect's duty to inspect the alignment of the panels.

Sheldon & others v RHM Outhwaite Ltd (1996)

In 1992, the claimants (all of whom were Lloyd's Names) brought proceedings against the defendants for negligence, breach of contract and breach of fiduciary duty.

The defendants contested that their actions were time-barred, such breaches having occurred in or around 1982. The claimants responded by contending that relevant facts to their causes of action had been deliberately concealed by the defendants in 1984 and, accordingly, limitation did not expire until six years following the discovery of such concealment.

The House of Lords held that *Limitation Act* 1980, section 32(1)(b) applied in circumstances where a deliberate concealment of relevant facts took place after the accrual of a cause of action. Lord Browne-Wilkinson, in delivering the leading judgment, explained that any other construction of the Act:

> '... would lead to an unfair result inconsistent with the underlying rationale of the section, viz. that the defendants would be entitled to benefit from their own unconscionable behaviour by deliberately concealing the facts relevant to the plaintiffs' cause of action'.

Cave v Robinson Jarvis & Rolf (2003)

The defendants were a firm of solicitors who, in March 1989, acted on behalf of the claimant to obtain mooring rights for 100 years over land in the Isle of Wight which belonged to a third party company. In 1994, receivers of the company's bank informed the claimant that his mooring rights were no longer exercisable. In March 1996, the District Land Registry informed the claimant that his mooring rights were not entered on the Land Register. The claimant issued proceedings against the defendants in January 1998.

The House of Lords held that the claimant's action was statute-barred. Where a defendant is unaware of an error or of a failure to take reasonable care, then such conduct cannot be brought within *Limitation Act* 1980, section 32(2) so as to prevent time from running until the discovery of the same.

As Lord Millett put it (at 395):

> 'The maxim that ignorance of the law is no defence does not operate to convert a lawyer's inadvertent want of care into an intentional tort.'

However, if a party inadvertently acts in breach of contract or duty but later realises that he has done so and fails to inform the party who may be affected by such a breach, then that party is likely to be able to prove that such an error has been deliberately or recklessly concealed from him and rely on *Limitation Act* 1980, section 32 if the primary limitation period has already expired.

11.5.1 Summary

- The underlying policy of the *Limitation Act* 1980 is that a claim must be brought within a reasonable period.

- The position is different where facts relevant to a claimant's cause of action are deliberately concealed by the defendant.

- Time will not run until the claimant discovers concealment or should with reasonable diligence have discovered it.

- Time will run from the moment when fraud, concealment or mistake is discovered or could reasonably have been discovered.

- In determining whether the concealed breach of duty could have been reasonably discovered, it may be relevant to consider whether the works were supervised. The defects will not be judged to have been 'concealed' if they would have been obvious upon a reasonable inspection. But this is a question of fact in each case – the mere existence of a supervisory body does not automatically let the builder off the hook.

11.6 DURATION OF THE CONTRACT ADMINISTRATOR'S DUTIES

In the absence of express agreement to the contrary, if a contract administrator is employed to arrange and supervise the building of specified works, he has the right and duty to continue acting until completion of the works.

A professional consultant who undertakes design obligations usually has a duty to keep that design under review and if necessary amend it up till the date of practical completion.

Wilson v Le Fevre Wood & Royle (1995)

This dispute arose out of building works to repair the plaintiff's bungalow. The defendant architects and surveyors were responsible for supervising the works. Works commenced in September 1982 and were completed by early 1983. It emerged that the building works were defective in that the building had serious problems with rising damp. From 1983 onwards, the plaintiff repeatedly complained to the defendant about the damp. On 8 March 1984 the defendant made its last inspection of the plaintiff's premises. On 9 March 1987 the plaintiff made a renewed complaint to the defendant, who declined to deal with it.

On 16 July 1990 the plaintiff commenced proceedings against the defendants. The writ was issued more than six years after the defendants' alleged negligence.

The Court of Appeal held that the claim was statute-barred. On the facts, it was held that the plaintiff owner had knowledge of the damage more then three years before the issuing of the writ. Only if the plaintiff owner established the requisite knowledge after 16 July 1987 would the claim be in time. The Court of Appeal held that the plaintiff owner had the requisite knowledge prior to this date.

In the case of a contractor, architect or engineer who undertakes responsibility for design, he may well have a duty to continue to monitor and revise that design throughout the period of the works up to the date of practical completion.

Equitable Debenture Assets Corporation Ltd v William Moss Group Ltd (1984)

The plaintiffs, who were developers of an office block in Ashford, sued their contractor, architect and others when the curtain walling on the completed building failed causing significant leaks.

In the action against the architect, the court held that an architect owes a duty to his client not only to produce his original design with reasonable skill and care but also to keep the design under review during construction. The duty to carry out a redesign as and when necessary was non-delegable without the plaintiffs' consent. Whilst the original decision to use curtain walling was not negligent, the architects were held to have been negligent in the selection of the curtain walling subcontractor, the approval of the subcontractor's detailed design, the unsystematic use of a curtain walling consultant and in their supervisory duties.

London Borough of Lewisham v MR Limited (2003)

The claimant entered into a contract with a construction company for building works to two residential tower blocks. Part of the works included overcladding (manufactured by the defendant), such works being commenced in January 1996 and completed by October 1996. The defendant (who had no contractual relationship with the claimant) inspected the overcladding works in August and September 1996.

Practical completion was retrospectively certified as having occurred on 8 November 1996. On 12 May 2003, the claimant brought proceedings against the defendant, claiming the costs of remedial works to rectify defects which had manifested themselves in the overcladding.

HHJ Bowsher QC held that the cause of action against the defendant manufacturer accrued from when he failed to properly supervise the subcontractor during inspections. Unlike the contract administrator, the defendant manufacturer's duties did not continue until practical completion of the works.

PART 4:
Duties Owed to Contract Administrators

12
Co-operation and right to payment

As ever, the rights enjoyed by a contract administrator will depend on the facts of each case and the terms of each contract. However, in the absence of an express agreement, the bare minimum duties that will be impliedly undertaken by an employer to a contract administrator include a duty to provide reasonable co-operation and a duty to pay a reasonable fee for his work.

12.1 CO-OPERATION

In the absence of an express agreement to the contrary, the contract administrator is entitled to expect that his employer will provide reasonable co-operation to allow him to carry out his duties and will not hinder or prevent him from doing so.

London Borough of Merton v Leach (1985)

There is an implied term in a contract that each party will not do anything to prevent the other party from performing the contract or to delay him in performing it. Of course, this may be qualified by an express term of the contract or by a fact to be inferred from the contract or the surrounding circumstances. However, it is difficult to conceive of a situation where this duty could be wholly excluded as, whilst parties are free to make whatever bargains they wish, such bargains must retain the legal characteristics of a contract in order to be enforceable.

There is also an implied duty that parties to a contract will do whatever is reasonably necessary in order to enable the other party to perform his obligations under the contract. However, there is no general, implied requirement to act in good faith: only that the parties should co-operate sufficiently to make the contract workable.

Thomas v Hammersmith Borough Council (1938)

In the normal course of events there will be an implied term of the contract administrator's engagement that the employer will not prevent him from doing the work he contracted to do and hence earning his remuneration. Put another way, the employer is bound to continue a state of things which is necessary to the carrying out of the contract.

12.2 RIGHT TO PAYMENT

The parties will usually make an express agreement as to how the contract administrator is to be remunerated for his work and by how much. However, in the absence of such an agreement, the contract administrator will usually be deemed to be entitled to a reasonable sum (a 'quantum meruit') for the work that he carries out. The question of what that reasonable sum might be is a matter of fact to be deduced from the circumstances of each case.

Bryant v Flight (1839)

In the absence of an express agreement, a contract administrator will be entitled to be paid a reasonable sum for the work he carries out.

The plaintiff had agreed to provide managerial services to the defendant on terms that the amount of payment he was to receive was left entirely to the defendant to determine. A majority of the Court of Exchequer of Pleas held that, the services having been proved to have been performed and to have been of value to the defendant, the plaintiff was entitled to recover reasonable compensation for them. The plaintiff had not said that he would leave it to the defendant to say whether he was to be paid anything or nothing; it was clear from the terms of the letter that he agreed to perform the services in the expectation that he would receive some remuneration and the only thing left open was the amount.

Way v Latilla (1937)

Where there have been inconclusive negotiations as to fees, the court will imply a term that the contract administrator is entitled to recover a reasonable sum for his work. Lord Atkin set out the legal principle as follows (p. 764):

'Services of this kind are no doubt usually the subject of an express contract as to remuneration, which may take the form of a fee, but may also take the form of a commission share of profits, or share of proceeds calculated at a percentage or on some other basis. In the present case, there was no question of fee between the parties from beginning to end. On the contrary, the parties had discussed remuneration on the footing of what may loosely be called a 'participation' and nothing else. The reference is analogous to the well known distinction between salary and commission. There are many employments the remuneration of which is, by trade usage, invariably fixed on a commission basis. In such cases, if the amount of the commission has not been finally agreed, the quantum meruit would be fixed after taking into account the bargainings between the parties, not with a view to completing the bargain for them, but as evidence of the value which each of them puts upon the services. If the discussion had ranged between 3 percent on the one side and 5 percent on the other, all else being agreed, the court would not be likely to depart from somewhere about those figures and would be wrong in ignoring them altogether and fixing remuneration on an entirely different basis, upon which possibly the services would never had been rendered at all.'

Brewin v Chaimberlain (1949)

Birkett J had to consider what was a reasonable sum to be paid to an architect for carrying out only part of his services where there was no express agreement as to how such a sum should be calculated. The employer argued that the fee should be calculated on the basis of a daily rate; the architect argued that it should be assessed as a percentage of the estimated cost of works which had been abandoned.

Both contentions were rejected: the time basis was inappropriate because it failed to take account of the value of architectural inspiration inherent in the work; the percentage basis was also too narrow in the factors to which it had regard.

The judge set out a list of the relevant factors to be taken into account when assessing a reasonable fee. He held that both the time spent and the fact that there was a term that limited the recoverable fee to a maximum percentage were relevant factors to be taken into account. Other relevant factors were the complexity of the job; the standard and merit of the drawings prepared; the standing and experience of the architect; and the amount and nature of the work required.

Under the *Housing Grants, Construction and Regeneration Act* 1996, a 'construction contract' is defined as including an agreement to do architectural, design or surveying work or to provide advice on building, engineering, interior or exterior decoration or on landscaping in relation to construction operations: see section 104(2). Accordingly, where a contract administrator's employment falls within that definition, the provisions of the Act (such as those relating to stage payments and the right to suspend work for non-payment) will apply.

12.3 RIGHT TO PAYMENT WHEN A PROJECT IS ABANDONED

Parties may expressly agree that the contract administrator's right to payment is contingent on the happening of an event such as the acceptance of a contractor's tender or the grant of planning permission by a local authority. In such circumstances, if the relevant event does not occur, the contract administrator will not be entitled to a fee for the work he carries out.

Where there is no such express agreement, the contract administrator may be able to persuade the court to imply a right to payment for his aborted work.

Moffatt v Laurie (1855)

There is a presumption that a contract administrator is entitled to be paid something for his work as it is reasonably to be inferred that people who do work for others expect to be paid for it. However, the parties had agreed that the plaintiff architect would make no charge for the provision of his services (surveys, plans etc) unless the land in question should be sold for building purposes, in which case he would be appointed architect for the works and be paid a fee.

Accordingly, on an action by the architect for the recover of a fee for the work he had done, the claim was rejected because the event which would have triggered an entitlement to payment had not happened.

Whipham v Everitt (1990)

An architect successfully recovered a fee for his preliminary work based on the RIBA scale, notwithstanding that there had been no express agreement with the employer to that effect.

The project was not taken forward after the failure to obtain a suitable tender. However, the court accepted expert evidence to the effect that it was customary in such circumstances for the architect to be paid a reasonable sum for the work he had completed. The contemporary RIBA scale of fees (now replaced by indicative fee arrangements in the 'Client's Guide to Engaging an Architect' published by RIBA) was not binding in law because it was not a custom of sufficiently universal application to be implied into all relevant construction contracts. However, the court held it was right to have regard to the usual practice in the profession.

12.4 PAYMENT FOR EXTRA WORK

Gilbert & Partners v Knight (1968)

In this case a surveyor agreed to prepare drawings, tenders and supervise alteration works to a residential property. The surveyor estimated the cost of the works at roughly £600 for which he would charge a fee of £30. When the builder started work, the employer ordered considerable extra work which brought the total cost to £2,283. The surveyor supervised the additional work but did not say anything about an additional fee for doing so until after the work had finished.

The court upheld the employer's case that she was only obliged to pay the agreed £30 fee. Although the fee was agreed in relation only to the work originally estimated and possible extras to it, no charge by way of quantum meruit for supervising the additional work was recoverable unless a new contract to pay a fee in respect of that work could be implied and no such implication could be made because the pre-existing agreement had never been discharged. In order to make a person liable on a quantum meruit, there has to be a necessary implication that the person liable is agreeing to pay. In this case, the old contract based on a lump sum was still subsisting and, in the absence of an indication to the contrary from the surveyor, the employer was entitled to assume that she would not be asked for a different sum on a different basis.

Where there is an express agreement as to the amount of a contract administrator's remuneration, the contract administrator may not be entitled to a reasonable sum or any additional fees for extra work unless he informs the employer at the time that he undertakes to carry out the extra work.

12.5 SUMMARY

- The contract administrator's rights will be defined by the facts of each case and by the terms of any contract that is agreed.

- In the absence of express words to the contrary, a term will be implied into the contract administrator's engagement that he shall be entitled to a reasonable sum for the work he carries out.

- The amount of such a reasonable sum is to be assessed by reference to all the circumstances, including any negotiations between the parties themselves and the nature of the work.

- The employer will be expected to co-operate with his contract administrator to the extent that is reasonably necessary to enable the latter to do his job and he must not hinder or prevent the contract administrator's work.

- The contract administrator may not be entitled to be paid in respect of additional or preparatory work if it is not possible to imply from the facts of the particular case an agreement to that effect.

PART 5:
Disputes and Dispute Resolution

13
Dispute resolution options available to the contract administrator

A thorough analysis of the different methods of dispute resolution which may be open to a party to a construction contract is beyond the scope of this text. However, summarised here are the options which a contract administrator may find himself involved with in the context of a dispute between members of the project team, the contractor, and possibly himself.

13.1 THE CONTRACT ADMINISTRATOR AS 'ARBITRATOR'

We have already seen in Parts 2 and 3 above that the contract administrator may assume a quasi-judicial or arbitral role in exercising a number of his functions under the contract. In matters such as certification and valuation he will be expected to act independently and fairly. This duty should not be underestimated; sometimes the issue of a certificate will be 'conclusive' and deprive the client of a remedy against a negligent contractor (see cases at 6.1 above). Further, a failure to act impartially may negate any decisions made by the contract administrator and risk incurring liability to the client.

13.2 MEDIATION

It is becoming more and more frequent to see mediation provisions inserted into construction contracts, whether bespoke or standard form. Such provisions are not necessarily binding; rather they tend to be inserted as a suggestion to the parties in an attempt to prevent disputes coming before a tribunal, which will inevitably prove more time-consuming and costly.

It is thought that provisions compelling a party to mediate would be contrary to the adjudication provisions of the *Housing Grants, Construction and Regeneration Act* 1996, which provides that a party should have the right to refer a dispute to adjudication at any time.

13.3 ADJUDICATION

Following the enactment of the *Housing Grants, Construction and Regeneration Act* 1996, many disputes under qualifying 'construction contracts' (as to which, see 1.4 above) fall to be determined, at least in the first place, by adjudication proceedings. Indeed, it is increasingly common for a dissatisfied party to tire of taking proceedings beyond the interim decision of the adjudicator, especially where it has already failed to challenge the enforcement of the decision on jurisdiction or natural justice grounds.

The ways in which adjudicator's awards can be challenged are the subject of a large body of case-law and is dealt with in another instalment of the Case in Point Series.

However, recent case-law has shown that a construction professional may well be under a duty of care when advising on contracts which contain adjudication provisions, and it is suggested that a contract administrator should be particularly aware of the following cases.

Picardi v Cuniberti (2003)

This case concerned construction works carried out at a property in West London. The contract did not come within the ambit of the *Housing Grants, Construction and Regeneration Act* 1996 because the employer was a residential occupier. The employer engaged an architect under the RIBA form of contract, the terms of which had been proffered by the architect. Adjudication proceedings were brought against the employer, who sought (at enforcement stage) to argue that as he was a 'consumer' within the meaning of the *Unfair Terms in Consumer Contract Regulations* 1999, the adjudication provisions of the RIBA form were unfair and were thus unenforceable against him. The court agreed (albeit in passing).

Lovell Projects Limited v Legg (2003)

This case concerned the enforcement of an adjudication brought under the JCT agreement for minor building works (1998 edition), which a residential occupier (as a 'consumer') sought to resist on the grounds that they were 'unfair'. HHJ Moseley QC held that the adjudication provisions of the JCT agreement for minor building works did not cause a significant imbalance in the parties' rights, were fully, clearly and legibly set out, and, as a result, were not in breach of the *Unfair Terms in Consumer Contract Regulations* 1999.

The critical difference between this case and *Picardi v Cuniberti* was that the standard form in question (which contained the adjudication provision) was proffered by or on behalf of the resisting party.

For other decisions distinguishing *Picardi v Cuniberti* on the same grounds, see *Westminster Building Company Limited v Beckingham* (2004); *Bryen & Langley Limited v Boston* (2005); and *Allen Wilson Shopfitters v Buckingham* (2005).

In *Lovell Projects v Legg* and *Westminster v Beckingham*, the terms of the contract were decided upon by a party's agent (namely an architect and a chartered surveyor respectively) before being proffered to the contractor.

In such circumstances it is not open to that party to subsequently contend that the same were 'unfair'. Instead, the authorities make it clear that any grievance that the 'consumer' may subsequently have as to the selection of the contract, its terms and/or operation, should be directed at his agents as advisors, who were in a position to provide advice in respect of the same. Such advice may of course fall under the ambit of the contract administrator's remit.

13.3.1 Position under JCT 2005

The JCT 2005 contract for minor works (with or without design ('MW/MWD')) and for intermediate works (with or without design ('IC/ICD')) may well be used by parties who fall within the definition of 'residential occupiers' for the purposes of *Housing Grants, Construction and Regeneration Act* 1996, section 106. As a result, the accompanying guides to each contract published by the JCT contain the following 'health warning':

IC 2005

'107 Care needs to be taken where an Intermediate Building Contract is used for a contract with a residential occupier within the meaning of section 106 HGRA 1996...

108 Since Part II of that Act does not apply to contracts with residential occupiers, as defined, the Employer's Architect or contract administrator may be under a duty to advise his or her client(s) accordingly, in particular with regard to adjudication and as to whether or not to disapply Article 7 and clause 9.2.'

MW 2005

'6 The Contract complies with the requirements of the Housing Grants, Construction and Regeneration Act 1996 in providing for adjudication and certain payment provisions; however, not all building contracts are subject to this Act. For example, a contract with a residential occupier within the meaning of section 106 of the Act is excluded and therefore it does not need to contain adjudication provisions, but a residential occupier in entering into a Minor Works Building Contract will be accepting adjudication as a means of resolving disputes.'

13.4 ARBITRATION

Many standard form contracts contain arbitration clauses which provide for the final determination of disputes thereunder to be settled by a private arbitral tribunal. Decisions of such tribunals are not usually made public, and it was once thought that arbitration proceedings provided swifter and more cost-effective justice. Whether or not this is still the case depends on the dispute and on the arbitrator, but it is increasingly doubtful.

A contract administrator should be aware that where a contract contains an arbitration clause, and litigation proceedings are issued against one of the parties, that party may insist that the proceedings be stayed to arbitration. Care should be taken to avoid taking a 'step' in the litigation proceedings (such as serving a defence) as this will have the effect of acceding to the court's jurisdiction. The decision of an arbitrator is final save as to questions of law, and even then, leave to appeal is exercised sparingly. It is open to the parties to contract out of a right to appeal.

13.5 LITIGATION

Litigation in the construction field is undergoing a resurgence in popularity following recent reforms of the Technology and Construction Court. Litigation is now the default form of dispute resolution under the JCT 2005 suite of contracts; if arbitration is desired then this must be expressly stated in the contract particulars.

Index

The *Case in Point* series

The *Case in Point* series is a popular set of concise practical guides to legal issues in land, property and construction. Written for the property professional, they get straight to the key issues in a refreshingly jargon-free style.

Areas covered:

Negligence in Valuation and Surveys
Stock code: 6388
Published: December 2002

Party Walls
Stock code: 7269
Published: May 2004

Service Charges
Stock code: 7272
Published: June 2004

Estate Agency
Stock code: 7472
Published: July 2004

Rent Review
Stock code: 8531
Published: May 2005

Expert Witness
Stock code: 8842
Published: August 2005

Lease Renewal
Stock code: 8711
Published: August 2005

VAT in Property and Construction
Stock code: 8840
Published September 2005

Construction Adjudication
Stock code: 9040
Published October 2005

Dilapidations
Stock code: 9113
Published January 2006

Planning Control
Stock code: 9391
Published April 2006

Building Defects
Stock code: 9949
Published July 2006

If you would like to be kept informed when new *Case in Point*
titles are published, please e-mail **rbmarketing@rics.org.uk**

All RICS Books titles can be ordered direct by:

- ☎ Telephoning 0870 333 1600 (Option 3)
- 🖰 Online at www.ricsbooks.com
- 📠 E-mail mailorder@rics.org.uk